Confused Men, Frustrated Women

CARL SNYDER

WESTBOW
PRESS®
A DIVISION OF THOMAS NELSON
& ZONDERVAN

WestBow Press books may be ordered through booksellers or by contacting:

WestBow Press
A Division of Thomas Nelson & Zondervan
1663 Liberty Drive
Bloomington, IN 47403
www.westbowpress.com
1 (866) 928-1240

Scripture quotations taken from the King James Version of the Bible.

ISBN: 978-1-9736-7072-8 (sc)
ISBN: 978-1-9736-7074-2 (hc)
ISBN: 978-1-9736-7073-5 (e)

Library of Congress Control Number: 2019911331

Print information available on the last page.

WestBow Press rev. date: 09/13/2019

Contents

Chapter 7: Concluding Observations................................ 93

Confused Men, Frustrated Women

For most people, it does not take long to discover that there are major differences between men and women. The differences can be seen as minor or major, depending on the relationship between the man and woman in question. The fact is, God created us different for good reasons. Each sex has qualities that are essential to navigating life. Finding that perfect balance between man and woman in the marriage relationship at first is taken for granted, but as the marriage progresses, it becomes very clear that it is a struggle to get it right. To a lesser degree, there is also a struggle between men and women not connected by marriage. The search for answers leads most people in the wrong direction. Secular psychologist are the preferred source, but they fail to deliver real and lasting help. God is the one who created us, and it is God who has provided the instruction manual. The best argument comes from results; the secular wisdom the world offers falls far short, while the wisdom of God produces lasting results that produce harmony and peace in our lives and relationships. This book will look at what the scriptures teach concerning the role of men and women, their relationship to each other, and the four basic conflicts we all face. From the biblical record, one can seek out and discover God's plan and purpose.

Perhaps this journey through the scriptures will help some

who are seeking meaning, purpose, and direction for their lives. All of us have asked the same old questions: "Why do people *act* as they do? Why do things *happen* as they do? How can I *change* things? How can I *change* people? How can I *change* myself?" For the majority of people in the world, the answers will never come. They have no idea where to look for answers to these questions, or they are looking in the wrong places. The struggle is to identify the problem and then find the biblical solution God has provided.

If you are like most people, you probably see things in two categories: the spiritual and the secular. The two categories seem to be incompatible with each other. The following story probably illustrates how some of us view these two. A pastor was delivering a sermon, and to support his message, he referred to the authority of John's gospel, the epistles of Paul, and other biblical writings. The congregation seemed unmoved. One man yawned; another was talking to the person next to him. A woman in the next row was checking the contents of her purse. "As Dr. Phil says …," the pastor continued. Instantly, a visible stir of attention rippled through the crowd as they strained forward to catch every word. The yawning man closed his mouth, and the woman shut her purse; both became very attentive. Dr. Phil, the one on television. Of course! If anyone knew the answers to the riddles of life, it would be Dr. Phil, a prominent psychologist. Unfortunately, Dr. Phil went through a nasty divorce that became very public.

It seems that we try to live in two different worlds at the same time: the spiritual and the secular. In addition, we try to utilize two different faiths: one faith in God and another in psychology and science—faith in God for spiritual matters and psychology and science for secular. The problem is trying to separate them. We generally look to psychology and science for matters pertaining to things we can see, hear, and touch. Spiritual faith is for matters unseen.

Christians have let their faith get entangled in a net of popular ideas about self-esteem and self-fulfillment that are not Christian ideas at all. For many, it is impossible to say where psychology leaves off and Christianity begins. In an attempt to get answers to life's questions, many have embraced a delusion that they can find happiness apart from God and have deepened their pain.

There are answers to life's questions and problems. In 2 Timothy 2:15, we read, "Study to show thyself approved unto God, a workman that needs not to be ashamed, rightly dividing the word of truth." We have some terrific promises given to us from God. In 2 Timothy 2:7, we are told, "For God has not given us the spirit of fear; but of power, and of love and of a sound mind." If you are a child of God by faith in Jesus Christ, that verse describes you!

The question now is, "Where do we begin?" In 1 Peter 3:7, we are told, "Likewise, you husbands dwell with them (wives) according to knowledge, giving honor unto the wife, as unto the weaker vessel, and as being heirs together of the grace of life; that your prayers be not hindered."

It is this knowledge that we need to seek and understand. This research will help develop the knowledge that 1 Peter is referring to. We will cover a wide range of information concerning God's design for man, God's organization, God's purpose in creation and its diversity, God's order for the family unit, and the issue of sin. The answers to these issues will be developed from the scriptures. There will not be any major argument to prove the biblical information, simply a presentation of what the Bible has to say on the issues set before us.

CHAPTER 1

God's Design

Man Is a Mystery

The more scientists study the human anatomy, the more marvelous it appears. The complexity of the human body continues to unfold with each new technology developed to study the human anatomy. Just when scientists think they have gathered all the data, new information is discovered.

Darwin repeatedly referred to the simple cell as the basic foundation of life. Much of what Darwin proposed was based on the simplistic design of the human cell. With the crude microscopes available at that time, the single cell looked similar to a round ball with a seed in the middle. Now we have discovered that the human cell is known to be extremely complex, made up of hundreds of thousands of smaller protein molecules. Harvard University paleontologist George Gaylord Simpson tells us that a single protein molecule is the most complicated substance known to humankind. A single cell is so complex that it boggles the minds of the scientists who have studied it.[1]

According to Psalm 8:5, humans are the crowning wonder

---

[1] James Kennedy, *Why I Believe* (Word Publishers, Dallas, 1980), p. 55.

of the universe. "For thou hast made him a little lower than the angels, and hast crowned him with glory and honour."

Man was also made in the likeness of God. "And God said, Let us make man in our image, after our likeness: and let them have dominion over the fish of the sea, and over the fowl of the air, and over the cattle, and over all the earth, and over every creeping thing that creeps upon the earth" (Genesis 1:26).

It would appear to many that there is more mystery in humans alone than in the whole universe. Humans are a walking example of the creative mind of God. We were created in the image of God, having emotion, intellect, and will, which is in contrast to the rest of creation. Adam did some damage to this resemblance due to the fall, but it can still be recognizable, according to 1 Corinthians 11:7, Acts 17:28, and James 3:9. The Genesis 1:26 account says that people were placed in authority over the creation and are clearly seen as superior to and dominate over the rest of creation. God's plan for humans was to subjugate and rule over His creation (Genesis 1:28). We read in Genesis 9:2 that God actually delivered everything into the control of humans. "And the fear of you and the dread of you shall be upon every beast of the earth, and upon every fowl of the air, upon all that moves upon the earth, and upon all the fishes of the sea; into your hand are they delivered."

Man also is self-centered, according to 2 Timothy 3:2. "For men shall be lovers of their own selves, covetous, boasters, proud, blasphemers, disobedient to parents, unthankful, unholy."

Philippians 2:21 says, "For all seek their own, not the things which are Jesus Christ's."

Man is a mystery even to his own thinking. "By thought and reasoning, man never comes to understand either his origin or himself."[2] History is full of examples of individuals trying to figure out the purpose for humans. The complexity of people has never been fully understood.

---

[2] C.B. Eavey, *Principles of Mental Health* (Moody Press, Chicago, 1973), p. 6.

Man Is a Body

Man has a body that was made out of the dust of the ground. Genesis 2:7 says, "And the LORD God formed man of the dust of the ground, and breathed into his nostrils the breath of life; and man became a living soul." This body that God created is made out of material, the dust of the ground, and it is active. It can perform functions, such as eating, sleeping, working, and playing, and has within its frame glands, nerves, muscles, blood, and so forth. The body contains energy for the purpose of generating motion, it is self-adapting to its environment (within limits), and it is self-maintaining by generating new cells and rebuilding tissue, thus producing a new body every seven years.[3] This amazing creation of God is also self-productive with the use of hands, feet, eyes, and mind. Humans can do what no other creature is capable of. Humans have designed and built structures that dwarf any nest, burrow, or dam built by lesser creatures.

Man Is a Living Soul

An interesting fact in all of this is the process God used. He first formed man out of the dust of the earth and then breathed into him the breath of life (Genesis 2:7). The Bible speaks of a person in terms of body, soul, and spirit. A human is referred to as a living soul in many passages. While many have struggled over the distinctions between the soul and the spirit, there are clearly some differences. The soul is the lower component of a person's makeup (James 3:13–18; Jude 19), while the spirit is the higher consciousness (Romans 8:16). The soul is directed toward the earthly and sensual (James 3:15), and the spirit is directed toward the divine and the supernatural. The soul aspires to self-consciousness, the spirit to God consciousness. It appears that the

---

[3] Ibid, p. 35.

soul is the connecting link between the body and the spirit. The soul entails our conscious feelings, knowledge, will, thoughts, affections, desires, and emotions.

Man Is a Spirit

The term *spirit* refers only to the immaterial part of a person, unlike *soul,* which can refer to the whole human—material and immaterial. A human is a soul, but a human is not said to be a spirit, yet he or she does possess a spirit.[4] The spirit originates from God, and all people have spirits (Numbers 16:22; Hebrews 12:9).

Though soul and spirit can relate to the same activities or emotions, there does seem to be a distinction and contrast between soul and spirit in Paul's writing. Humans certainly are a complicated piece of work.

Eric Sauer, in his work *Dawn of World Redemption,* gives his definition of humans. This definition seems to be comprehensive. "Man is a moral, indestructible personality, with self-consciousness, understanding, reason, a power of moral judgment, and freedom of will—to which is added his vocation to rule."

---

[4] Charles Ryrie, *Basic Theology* (Victor Books, United States, 1986), p. 197

CHAPTER 2

God's Organization

God Created the Human Race

The foundations for family life were put in place from the very beginning of God's creation. Shortly after God created the first man (Adam), He created a woman (Eve) and told them to be fruitful and multiply (Genesis 1:28). Humans were created distinct and separate from the animals. Although Adam and Eve were the last of God's creations, in order of importance, they were first. Adam (meaning "man") and Eve (meaning "mother of all") were the crowning glory of God's creation.

The creation of a man from the dust of the ground was a masterwork that only the omnipotent God could accomplish. No wonder the psalmist David could exclaim, "I will praise thee; for I am fearfully and wonderfully made: marvelous are thy works; and that my soul knoweth right well" (Psalm 139:14).

Nothing can compare to the wonder of the human body that God created. Nothing that humans have ever made can compare to the glory of God's masterpiece. No computer can compare to the human brain and no camera to the human eye. When people build an artificial heart, they can do no better than use the human heart as the pattern.

God Created Male and Female

"And the Lord God said, It is not good that the man should be alone; I will make him an help meet for him" (Genesis 2:18). The word *meet* means "fit." God gave Adam a helper "fit for him" or suitable for him." Today we often speak of a wife as her husband's helpmeet.

> Notice … that Adam was first formed, then Eve (1 Timothy 2:13) … If man is the head, she is the crown; a crown to her husband, the crown of visible creation. The man was dust refined, but the woman was dust double-refined, one removed further from the earth … [Notice] that the woman was made of a rib out of the side of Adam, not made out of his head to top him, not out of his feet to be trampled upon by him, but out of his side to be equal with him, under his arm to be protected and near his heart to be beloved. (Matthew Henry, XX)

It does not take a genius to discover that men and women are very different—physically and emotionally. The makeup of women is different from that of men. Women's skin is thinner, and they have less muscle. Right from birth, women have a better immune system (fewer female babies die at birth), and even their blood is different from men's. A man has about 1 million more red blood cells in every drop of blood and has 1.5 gallons compared to four-fifths of a gallon for women. That is the reason that men can work longer than women at hard labor. After about ten hours of hard labor, women begin to fall out. Their bodies are about 20 percent muscle, while men are 40 percent muscle. The extra blood also helps the man endure longer. Women have a layer of insulating cells all over their body that allows them to gain weight faster and lose it more slowly than men. Men have thicker skin, bones, and skulls.[5] A woman has a bilateral ability in the use of her brain. Men are lateral, one side at a time. Women have more connecting fibers going from one side to the other. This allows women to take in more information at any given moment. They hear more, see more, and remember more. If a message is flashed on a screen and everyone present is told to write down what they saw, the women would begin writing, while the men would say, "Did you see that?"

The male predominantly uses the left side of the brain, which is primarily for language, logic, and accounting. That is why men are generally less talkative than women. Women love to share feelings and to communicate emotions. This results in women tending to be more romantic and less aggressive. Men start fights and are generally more aggressive. In 1996, more than 100 million romance novels were purchased, and women bought 99.9 percent. In conversation, this shows up as a problem; women want to talk about their feelings, while men want to hear facts. A study was done with five-year-old children. The girls were put into one room and the boys in another room, and then they were recorded. For the girls, 100 percent of their response was conversational. They talked to themselves and to each other, but they were communicating words. The boys were very different; only 60 percent of their verbal efforts were in the form of conversation, while 40 percent was just noises, making sounds. The average woman will speak 25,000 words a day, while the average man will say about 12,000 words, but she is just beginning. [6]

God Created the Family Unit

God had the family in mind when He told Adam and Eve to be fruitful and multiply (Genesis 1:28). Children are the result of the

---

[5] John Gray, *Men Are from Mars Women Are from Venus* (Harper Collins, New York, 1992), p. 9.

[6] Ibid., p. 11.

"one flesh" experience. Starting with Adam and Eve, the family was in trouble. After the fall of humanity, sin entered the scene, creating some challenging problems for Adam and his descendants. In fact, his firstborn son, Cain, eventually killed his brother Abel.

When we talk about the problems of holding the family together, we assume certain ideas. The first assumption: the family unit is proper and normal. No matter where you go in the world, the family unit is present. If one would follow the logical thought pattern, the conclusion would suggest that we could trace our roots back to the same place. People have traditions and customs that have been passed on by their parents and grandparents. These traditions and customs are very different depending upon where you travel in the world. The one thing that is found everywhere is the family unit, suggesting that we all can trace that practice back to the same source. Adam and Eve would be a logical conclusion.

The second assumption: faithfulness in marriage is proper and right. But then we would have to ask, "Who set the standard?" Again, we find this idea common among all nations and people. This idea or practice is as old as marriage itself. The conclusion is simple: *in the beginning, God!*

In Genesis 2:1–25, we have the description of the beginning of family life. The family unit was in the garden; Adam and Eve were the first marriage. God brought Adam and Eve together prior to the fall, and marriage has been a part of the human race ever since. It is the family unit that gives purpose to everyday activity. The family unit provides for the nurturing of our young and the provision for our old. The family unit provides a means to pass on the truths we have learned to our young and to remember the accomplishments of our forefathers. Over the years, the family has stood at the center of civilization. But, as of the end of the twentieth century, the family is in trouble. Divorces almost equal viable marriages. We find couples living together without the sanction of marriage. We have lost sight of our heritage and wander aimlessly seeking a sense of fulfillment that will never be found. Our nation is in trouble. We are in the last stages of national decline.

God's Presence in the Family Is Essential to Its Survival

Over the years, it is possible to see a decline in values and morals in our country. Living through the changes makes it very difficult to see what is actually taking place. Looking back, we recognize that changes took place, but often we are obvious to the changes at the time they occur. A judge in the state of Indiana has identified and labeled the steps to national decline. He sees several stages or steps that can be identified on the road to decline. These steps are understandable when looked at from an analytical perspective.

Seven Steps to National Decline

1. Begins with **faith**   (Our founding fathers)
2. Which exercises **liberty**   (Our national freedom)
3. Which produces **abundance**   (Our gross national product)
4. Which leads to **selfishness**   (Our national goal, "Get all you can")
5. Which develops **complacency**   (Our national attitude)
6. Which gives birth to **apathy**   (Our national condition: "What's the use?")
7. Which produces **dependency**   (Guaranteed national wages)

—Judge William Obermiller[7]

The world says we came from slime. The scriptures say, "In the beginning God created." The world says, "Get all you can—you only go around once." The scriptures declare that if we want to receive, then we must give up; if we want to live, then we must die to self. The life of a believer in Christ Jesus is definitely different from the life the unsaved seek after. There is joy and satisfaction in

---

[7] Judge William Obermiller, city judge for Whiting, Indiana, from 1962-2000, Known as the spanking judge

serving the Lord. Psalm 29:11 says, "The Lord will give strength unto his people; the Lord will bless his people with peace."

We make a big mistake as Christians if we think we can live as the world does and still have "the peace that passes understanding." Paul writes in Romans 5:1, "Therefore being justified by faith we have peace with God through our Lord Jesus Christ." Paul also makes it clear that sinful disobedience will result in major problems. We read in Romans 6:16, "Know you not, that to whom you yield yourselves servants to obey, his servants you are to sin unto death, or of obedience unto righteousness?" Like it or not, peace and happiness ultimately depend on our relationship to the God who created us. When we rebel against what God has declared in His written word, we are simply complicating our lives and making life very difficult.

The beginning of understanding life is to understand what God has said about the world we live in and the people we live with. There are four basic foundations from the Bible that are critical to understand if we are going to have a biblical perspective on humanity.

1. **God** created the human race.
2. **God** created male and female
3. **God** planned the family unit.
4. **God's** presence in the family is essential to its survival.

The scriptures clearly state that God created the human race (Genesis 1:26–28). The general approach from the scientific community rejects the idea that God created humans and embraces the theory of evolution as the source of life. Are the choices before us simply evolution or creation? Where do you stand? I believe the answer is critical to your well-being.

Evolution is a philosophy, not a science. The general premise of organic evolution is the theory that all living things have arisen by a materialistic, naturalistic evolutionary process from a single source, which itself arose by a similar process from a dead, inanimate world. The creation account in Genesis, on the other hand, records the fact that all basic animal and plant types were brought into existence by acts of God using special processes that are not operative today.[8]

Most scientists accept evolution, not as a theory, but as an established fact. Theodosius Dobzhansky, geneticist and widely-known evolutionist, formerly professor of zoology at Columbia University and the University of California, Davis, has said that "The occurrence of the evolution of life in the history of the earth is established about as well as events not witnessed by human observers can be."[9] Richard B. Goldschmidt, a professor at the University of California, before his death, stated dogmatically that "Evolution of the animal and plant world is considered by all those entitled to be a fact for which no further proof is needed."[10]

Almost all modern science books and school and university texts present evolution as an established fact. This alone causes many people to accept this idea without question. The proponents of the evolution theory adamantly insist that special creation be excluded from any possible consideration as an explanation for origins on the basis that it does not qualify as a scientific theory. On the other hand, they would view as unthinkable the consideration of evolution as anything less than pure science.

For a theory to qualify as a scientific theory, events, processes, or properties, which can be observed, must support it, and the theory must be useful in predicting the outcome of future natural phenomena or laboratory experiments.

It is on the basis of such criteria that most evolutionists insist that creation be refused consideration as a possible explanation

---

[8] Michael Bere, *Bible Doctrines for Today* (Beka Books, Pensacola Christian College, 2004), p. 189.

[9] Theodosius Dobzhansky, *Genetics and the Origin of the Species* (Columbia Press, New York, 1951), p. 39.

[10] Edward Goldsmith, *The Basis of Evolution* (Yale University Press, 1952), p. 125.

for origins. The general theory of evolution also fails to meet all three of these criteria. While evolutionists deny the miraculous in the origin of living things, the evolutionary process, given enough time, supposedly produces miracles.

> Frog, given a kiss = prince = nursery tale
> Frog, given 300 million years = prince = science

It is often stated that there are no reputable scientists who do not accept the theory of evolution. This is just one more false argument to win converts. While it is true that creationists among scientists definitely constitute a minority, there are many creation scientists, and their number is growing. Among these are well-established scientists like Dr. A. E. Wilder-Smith, professor of pharmacology in Boggern, Switzerland; Dr. W. R. Thompson, world-famous biologist and former director of the Commonwealth Institute of Biological Control of Canada; Dr. Melvin A. Cook; Dr. Henry M. Morris at Virginian Polytechnic Institute and University; Dr. Walter Lammerts, geneticist and famous plant breeder, etc.

Without God at the center of the family unit, stability and longevity are lost. If you remove God from consideration, then the source and purpose of the family unit is gone. There remains no structure or control for the family unit if God is removed from its consideration. Removing God removes the source of marriage, the guiding principles of marriage, and its purpose. Without God, marriage is simply a creation of humans and is therefore open to change, modification, or elimination, which is what many are attempting to accomplish today.

CHAPTER 3

God's Purpose in Creation

Man's Purpose in Creation

"Male and female created He them" (Genesis 1:27). Genesis 1:26 says, "And God said, Let us make man in our image, after our likeness." This is reinforced in 1 Corinthians 11:7: "For a man indeed ought not to cover his head, forasmuch as he is the image and glory of God."

There are **four specific things** that God gave men to do. The first purpose for a man is to show what God is like to his children, wife, etc. In order to accomplish this, God has equipped men with a special ability, which is the ability to exhibit. This ability involves displaying, manifesting, demonstrating, and showing off. Men are just natural show-offs; this can be seen without any need for a college degree. Men are constantly saying, "Look at me! Look at how strong I am, how fast I can run, how much I can lift." They compare themselves to other men in areas of ability, strength, and accomplishments.

"We will not hide them from their children, showing to the generations to come the praises of the Lord, and His strength, and His wonderful works that he hath done" (Psalm 78:4).

"He commanded our fathers that they should make them known to their children" (Psalm 78:5).

This ability is often misapplied; men fail to understand what God intended it to be used for. The purpose of displaying is to show our families *how* to praise the Lord. We are to teach our families *how* the Lord delivered His people in the past, so they will have hope in the present. We are to remind our families *how* the Lord continues to do great things in our lives today.

"The living, the living, he shall praise thee, as I do this day; the father to the children shall make known thy truth" (Isaiah 38:19).

"We have heard with our ears, O God; our fathers have told us what work thou didst in their days in times of old" (Psalm 44:1).

"I will praise thee, O Lord, with my whole heart; I will show forth all thy marvelous works" (Psalm 9:1).

Therefore, men are created with the ability to show the glory of God to others, and it begins at home. The impact of a father who is accomplishing what God called him to do cannot be overestimated as to its value to the rest of the family.

The second purpose is found in Genesis 1:26: "Let them have dominion over all the earth." The purpose here is **to rule** over God's creation. In order to accomplish this, God has given men the ability to shoulder responsibility. Synonyms would be *rule, dominate, govern, control, administer,* or to exercise *authority, leadership, headship,* and *influence.*

"Thou made him to have dominion over the works of thy hands" (Psalm 8:6).

"Wives, submit yourselves unto your own husbands, as unto the Lord. For the husband is the head of the wife, even as Christ is the head of the church" (Ephesians 5:22, 23).

The results: men are to take charge for the overall well-being of the family. They are to protect their family from all threats, both real and imagined. The imagined part is very critical for men to understand. Women have been given a sixth sense from

God; they can sense things that men have no hint of. This ability will cause women to have a sense of danger or calamity when there is no evidence present. Men need to understand this and offer comfort and protection for the perceived danger that they cannot see or sense. Sometimes in the middle of the night, a wife may wake up with a sense of panic over something she cannot explain; that is the time for the husband to hold her, giving her a sense of protection. When the man responds in this manner, the woman will feel a sense of security and protection that will strengthen their relationship. If the man simply rolls over and says that everything is fine, he will isolate his wife and increase her sense of danger.

Men are to lead by example, setting the standard for godly living. Demanding a certain standard from the rest of the family, but failing to live it himself, will develop a lack of respect from other family members. Therefore, men are created with the ability to guide and rule their homes, churches, governments, and the environment by setting the example.

The third purpose is found in Genesis 1:28: "Be fruitful and multiply and fill the earth." The purpose is to produce offspring like him and fill the earth with children who know and serve the Lord. This special ability enables the man to reproduce himself. Since this requires the selection of a mate with whom to unite, and because of his physical structure, he must also be able to seek, find, love, and protect.

"Lo, children are a heritage from the Lord: and the fruit of the womb is his reward" (Psalm 127:3).

"As arrows are in the hand of a mighty man, so are children of one's youth" (Psalm 127:4).

"He that findeth a wife findeth a good thing" (Proverbs 18:22).

"So ought men to love their wives as their own bodies" (Ephesians 5:28).

Therefore, men are created with the ability to find a wife, love

15

her, protect her, become one flesh with her, and love and protect their children.

The fourth purpose is found in Genesis 2:15: "And put him in the garden … to dress it and to keep it." This purpose is for men to tend to God's creation and to provide for their families. The special ability is the ability to work. Synonyms include *labor, toil, exert energy, rough it, set his shoulder to the plow, perform, operate, achieve,* and *take action.*

"Six days shalt thou labor and do all thy works" (Exodus 20:9).

Deuteronomy 5:13 is the same command as Exodus 20:9.

"And to work with your own hands, as we commanded you" (1 Thessalonians 4:11).

"But if any provide not for his own, and especially for those of his own house, he hath denied the faith, and is worse than an infidel" (1 Timothy 5:8).

Therefore, men are created with the ability to work six days (rest one) and to have physical stamina to provide for their families year after year.

Women in Creation

The women's role is found in Genesis 2:18: "I will make him a help meet for him." In the Hebrew, it literally means a helper suitable for him, completing him, adaptable to him. There are three things involved with God's purpose for women.

The first purpose is to fit in with and "round out" the man. In order to do this, the woman is given a special **ability to adapt.** I have noticed a pattern that takes place over and over. When my wife and I would go away on vacation, some things were predictable. When we arrived at our destination, she would immediately start setting up our living space, if it was a cabin, she would arrange things; if it was a hotel, she would unpack our suitcases in an attempt to establish our space. Women have this built-in sense of home, how to make one and how to maintain one, adapting to any given situation. Synonyms for *adapt* include *adjust, accommodate, yield, understand, submit,* or to be *gracious, sensitive, reconcilable, dependent,* and *agreeable.*

"And thy desire shall be to thy husband, and he shall rule over thee" (Genesis 3:16).

"Wives submit to your own husbands, as unto the Lord" (Ephesians 5:22).

"Wives submit to your own husbands, as it is fit in the Lord" (Colossians 3:18).

"Let your women keep silence in the churches; for it is not permitted unto them to speak, but to be under obedience, as also saith the law" (1 Corinthians 14:34).

"Let the woman learn in silence with all subjection" (1 Timothy 2:11).

"But I permit not a woman to teach, nor to usurp authority over the man, but to be in silence" (1 Timothy 2:12).

"A gracious woman retaineth honor" (Proverbs 11:16).

"A virtuous woman is a crown to her husband" (Proverbs 12:4).

Women are created with the ability to adapt to men, especially their husbands, yielding to ordained authority. This is especially important when considering the fact that men tend to develop habits and refuse to bend or adjust. They become like old dogs; you cannot teach them new tricks.

The second purpose is found in Genesis 2:24: "Therefore shall a man leave his father and mother and cleave to his wife, and they shall be one flesh." The challenge for the woman is to get a man to be willing to leave home for her. After all, why should a man leave his home, where his mother cooks his meals and his father puts a roof over his head? There needs to be a special ability, and that is the **ability to attract** a man away from his parents.

Synonyms for this ability include three progressive sets of words:

    a. To pull, magnetize, and charm
    b. To allure, tempt, and tantalize
    c. To excite love, affection, and worship

"In like manner, also, that woman adorn themselves in modest apparel [well arranged] with Godly fear and sobriety [well balanced state of mind], not with braided hair [elaborate hairstyles] or with gold, or pearls, or costly array [jewelry]" (1 Timothy 2:9).

The Song of Solomon 4:1–6 describes the natural beauty of the woman apart from all the elaborate makeup. There is a natural beauty that God has given to women, and this is what needs to be understood and put to the proper use.

Therefore, women are created with the ability to attract the male. To do this properly, she must respect (reverence) the man she is attracting.

> Nevertheless, let everyone of you in particular so love his wife even as himself; and the wife, see that she reverences her husband. (Ephesians 5:33)

> In the same manner, ye wives be in subjection to your own husbands that; if any obey not the word, they also may without the word be won by the behavior of the wives. While they behold your chaste conduct coupled with fear; whose adorning let it not be that outward adorning of braiding the hair, and of wearing of gold, or of putting on of apparel; but let it be the hidden man of the heart in that which is not corruptible, even the ornament of a meek and quiet spirit, which is in the sight of God of great price. (1 Peter 3:1–4)

The third purpose for women is the same as found for man in Genesis 1:28: "Be fruitful and

multiply and fill the earth." The purpose is to
produce offspring like herself and fill the earth
with children who know and serve the Lord. The
special ability is the ability to reproduce herself.

Synonyms for this ability include *propagate, generate, produce children, feed and care for others, be a mother.* The requirements are that she must receive the male seed and carry a fetus till birth (this creates a special relationship between mother and child). Her special abilities include the following:

a. Handle emotional and physical changes
b. Bear discomfort and pain
c. Be patient, gentle, tender, sympathetic, devoted, affectionate, hospitable[11]

Ezekiel 19:10 implies that the hand that rocks the cradle rules the world. The world system tries to minimize the role of parenting for a woman. The impact of a mother's love and devotion to her children has been seen in the lives of countless people.

> I will, therefore, that the younger women marry, bear children, guide the house, and give no occasion to the adversary to speak reproachfully. (1 Timothy 5:14).

> The aged women likewise, that they be in behavior as becometh holiness, not false accusers, not given to much wine, teachers of good things, that they may teach the young women to be sober-minded, to love their husbands, to love their children, to be

---

[11] Jay Adams, *Solving Marriage Problems,* (Baker Books, Grand Rapids, Michigan, 1983), p. 21.

> discreet, chaste, keepers at home, good, obedient
> to their own husbands, that the word of God be
> not blasphemed. (Titus 2:3–5).

Therefore, women are created with the abilities to reproduce themselves, to be able to attract a man, to receive his seed, and to provide, through pregnancy, their own offspring.

Male Application

All men possess leadership tendencies, some more than others. Those with strong leadership abilities are called **SNLs** (Strong Natural Leaders).[12] SNLs make up about 25 percent of the total male population. Most are just average leaders, but every man has both the capability and the desire to be a leader, especially in his own home and marriage. This is a need that every man has, and if it is not fulfilled, it will in some cases cause him to act irrationally. This characteristic is one of the areas where men differ from most women. While some strong-willed women (cholerics) do enjoy leadership, they are in the minority. Most women would prefer the man to take the leadership role in the home.[13]

With a female-dominated home, you will find husbands to be irresponsible, wives frustrated, and children abnormal. With a man, work is a compulsion and productivity a necessity. Deep within men is the God-given drive to work, to accomplish, to be productive. Women often resent the fact that their husbands give more time and attention to their work than to them. Most men are more comfortable at work; they understand their role, and they understand what is needed and how to accomplish it. When they do well, they receive praise and sometimes monetary reward as well. It is easy for a man to be a leader at work; the requirements

---

[12] Tim LaHaye, *Understanding the Male Temperament* (Baker Books, Grand Rapids, Michigan, 1996), p. 17
[13] ibid., p. 27.

are clearly defined. However, when a man is at home, he often suffers from a lack of understanding of what is required of him; he is not sure how to handle his wife or his children, so he simply drifts off into his own world of sports, news, or some other source of activity. This leaves the wife feeling uncared for, unappreciated, and used. Men want to lead and they need to lead, but until they learn how to lead the way God intended, life will be very complicated for them.

God created men with the ability to work. Genesis 2:5 says, "there was no man to till the ground," so God made man with this intention in mind. After the creation of man and before the fall, God placed Adam in the Garden of Eden "to tend and keep it" (Genesis 2:15). God made man with the ability to work. There was no "free ride," even before sin entered into the picture.

After the fall, God's command to Adam was even more specific: "In the sweat of your face you shall eat bread" (Genesis 3:19). The first two children born on the Earth are mentioned in relation to their areas of work: "Abel was a keeper of sheep, and Cain was a tiller of the ground" (Genesis 4:2). For centuries, there was no confusion of roles; men were to be breadwinners, providers, and leaders of the home; women were to bear children and be "keepers at home." A large part of our problems today is simply due to a confusion of roles—what should the men do, and what should the women do?

God created men different from women, and one area where this can be identified is in the response to danger. All men have a basic ingredient to their makeup called courage. The amount will vary, but it is present in all men. It was this trait that made men the protectors of their families, homes, and countries. Courage is a trait both men and women possess, but tend to show differently. Women will courageously sacrifice themselves for their children, and history is full of examples. When threatened, a woman may throw her body over her child in protection; this is not necessarily so with a man—he would be more inclined to engage in combat with the one threatening his child.[14]

It is this courageous spirit of man that sent Columbus to sea to eventually discover America, the early American pioneers to settle the west, the astronauts to go to the moon, and countless others. It has pushed many to grasp the unreachable. It is this spirit that moves a man to accept challenge, to resist odds, to push limits.

Believe it or not, the mind of a man is different from that of a woman. This becomes apparent in childhood, when most little boys lose interest in dolls and go for the trucks, cars, and sports items while girls are still playing house. This difference is very clear in the area of sexual lust. When a boy reaches puberty, he starts to develop physically as a man and mentally cultivates an overwhelming interest in girls. At this stage of development, he is capable of lust to a degree that women find difficult to comprehend.

Easily the most beautiful, fascinating, and intriguing sight in most men's comprehension is the sight of a woman's body. This natural male weakness is related to his sex drive, which is linked to his manhood and must be kept under control. The primary means of control include marriage, a good character, and a strong spiritual life.[15] A good sex life in marriage can enable a man to control his sex drive and his thoughts, which, in turn, can improve his spiritual life (1 Corinthians 7:1–5).

Another mental area that is different between men and women is the man's goal-oriented thinking pattern. Women, by nature, tend to think vocationally of the home and the things that pertain to it, child-rearing, and the needs of her family. Men tend to become absorbed in their vocational pursuits. For a man, his means of livelihood can easily become the focal point of his life, especially if he likes his work. The result is that his home life suffers and he may even neglect fathering his children properly

---

[14] Ibid., p. 31.
[15] Marlin Savage, *The Four Conflicts in Marriage* (Unpublished Personal Notes, 1978).

22

at crucial times in their lives. Most men need to periodically take an objective look at their children and, on occasion, restructure their priorities in order to accommodate their fatherhood responsibilities. The man that allows his work to take priority over his family will live to regret it.

Men are probably not as emotional as women of the same temperament combinations, whether choleric, melancholy, sanguine, or phlegmatic. Women tend to have more outward signs of emotion than men; that does not mean men do not. Men do possess strong feelings, but most men tend to internalize them. This creates a sense in women that men are insensitive or simply do not care. This difference often results in conflict between men and women involved in crisis.

Scientists tell us that we each have an emotional center that is neurologically tied to every organ in the body. All physical action starts in the emotional center. If a person is upset, his or her condition originates in the emotional center and is carried to other areas of the body. A tense person is so susceptible to all kinds of physical diseases.[16]

Feelings are not spontaneous. They are the result of your thoughts. If your thoughts are good, so will be your feelings. Do you want to change your feelings? Then change your thoughts, and gradually your feelings will change.[17]

Generally, women have a greater capacity for love and affection than men do. In fact, a woman's love has a height, depth, breadth, and strength that will confuse most men. Men have to work at showing love far more than women do. Four times the Bible commands men to love their wives, where it only indirectly addresses women.[18]

---

[16] S. I. McMillen and David E. Stern, *None of These Diseases* (Baker Books, Grand Rapids, Michigan, 2000), p. 169.+

[17] Ibid., p. 173.

[18] John Gray, *Men Are From Mars Women Are From Venus* (Harper Collins, New York, 1992), p. 133.

Women need to learn to accept this male weakness and avoid becoming bitter when men's love for sports, business, or anything else seems to outweigh their love for women. Every married man should seek God's help in deepening his love for his wife. Men need to learn to do what comes naturally to women—to show love and affection.

I do not have to point out the obvious differences, but there are some that may not readily be so apparent. Men need regular physical exercise. Their bodies were designed for hard work and physical exercise. When men are active in physical exercise, they are less stressed and tend to be healthier longer.[19] Sweat-producing activity will usually give a man vitality around the house as well. The body will crave what you give it; exercise can become addictive in a sense, but so is laziness. A well-exercised man will be more attentive to doing things around the house that involve strength because he will have more energy as a result of his exercise. A scientific fact: things in motion tend to stay in motion, and things at rest tend to stay at rest.

Even when it comes to the sex act, men and women are different. The sex drive in a man is generally stronger than in women. It is difficult to exaggerate the role of man's sexuality in his makeup; it is an important source of his masculinity, manliness, chivalry, and aggressiveness. A man is stimulated by sight, and it doesn't take much to accomplish this. Women respond to touch, caresses, hugs, and verbal expressions of compassion. For the first thirty-five years, men tend to be the aggressors; after thirty-five, women tend to be the aggressors. This seems to be God's way of keeping the "one flesh" experience important in the marriage relationship (1 Corinthians 7:5).

Men will give affection to get sex; a woman will give sex to get affection. Take away a man's sex drive, and he will go into neutral.

---

[19] S. I. McMillen and David E. Stern, *None of These Diseases* (Baker Books, Grand Rapids, MICHIGANichigan, 2000), p. 193.

Eunuchs rarely are outstanding in any field. While there are examples, such as Daniel, these are rare. However, with Daniel, we see what God can do in the life of an individual dedicated to Him.

An often-quoted comment points out the female confusion on this subject: "Men are sexual animals." This statement is wrong on two counts: men are not animals, and they are not abnormal, as the comment suggests. All normal men have a strong sexual drive. Individual temperament will determine the manner of expressing sexuality.[20]

One difference between men and women that causes undue pain, especially in the early years of marriage, is in the way they are aroused sexually. A woman usually enjoys a long buildup to sexual activity that includes affectionate interchanges, tenderness, and kind acts of affection. She enjoys a long, slow approach.

Men are different, of course. A man is moved by sight, which quickly moves through his brain to his emotional center and directly to his sex organs. Unless he learns self-control, and his wife learns that his passion is really his way of showing love and affection, they will have a hard time communicating their needs.

Behind every man's complex nature is a little, fun-loving boy. Sooner or later, the little boy will show up. Some men are practical jokers; others are lovers of excitement. Some believe they are still the star football or baseball players they were in high school. Some perceive the freeway to be a glorified version of a racetrack. Others enjoy sporting events where they can imagine themselves out on the field.[21]

The boy in every man makes him seek some element of excitement. For some, it is contact sports, hunting, fishing, or some other form of competition. Many women get upset over the intensity of the competition between men.

---

[20] Tim LaHaye, *Understanding the Male Temperament* (Baker Books, Grand Rapids, Michigan, 1996), p. 196.
[21] Ibid., p. 223.

Have you ever noticed how young fathers like to give their sons toys that they can play with themselves? Although some men may indulge their "boy within" so much that they never grow up, they will normally use it for a welcome diversion. That's what makes him play so hard on a holiday that he can barely pull his stiff, aching body out of bed to go to work the next day. It may be hard for wives to understand, but the boy in every man is what makes him a sports lover. If your husband's indulgence of his boyish nature is indeed excessive, your heavenly Father knows it. He will fight for you by convicting your husband and giving you grace. Though it will take practice on your part, submission will be worth it in the long run as you build a sound marriage relationship. You cannot change the man (or the boy) you are married to, but God can! Give Him time.

Female Application

A survey was conducted to understand what makes for a happy marriage. When the results were in, the answers were predictable: "All we need is love." Most men know this is true, but doing something about it is the hard part. The results that came in were fascinating. No matter where couples live and regardless of economic or social standings, there are common threads that can run through all marriages. Among some of the highlights:

- People seem to have the same problems in their marriages, no matter how long they've been married.
- People tend to be more forgiving of each other the longer they have been married.
- No one has a perfect marriage.
- Husbands are quite transparent and knowledgeable about their inadequacies.
- Wives, by and large, are forgiving of their husbands, but also understand their faults clearly.

Without a doubt, there is a common thread when it comes to the top issue that creates conflict and difficulty in marriage: a woman's need for love.

Once the research was complete, the obvious became very clear: love is the key. Unfortunately, the word *love* is used for everything from "I love nachos" to "Of course I love you." Men understand love in terms much different from women. Men tend to depend on words, while women definitely need action to validate any love statement.

A number of husbands were asked the following question: "What do you think is your wife's number one need that you should fulfill?" Here is a sampling of answers, which became a constant chorus:

"I find that the quicker my wife and I can get off the surface behaviors to the underlying issues, the better we progress. The greatest single need of my wife is to be loved. I guess Paul had it right in Ephesians 5!"

"Two words sum up her greatest need: *affection* and *attention*."

"She needs my continual love and acceptance."

"She needs to be cherished, not just through words (although they are critical), but through thought and deed."

This is just a sampling, but plenty enough to see a steady theme of love and affection that comes through loud and clear. Unfortunately, as anticipated, though the survey asked an equal number of questions—three each—of wives and husbands, the majority of the responses came back from women. Of course men are too busy for such silly things as questionnaires—especially when those questions have to do with such an often guilt-ridden area as their own marriage relationships![22]

---

[22] Hans and Donna Finzel, *The Top Ten Ways to Drive Your Wife Crazy* (Victor Books, United States, 1984), p. 23.

Affection Is the Cement of a Relationship

To most women, affection symbolizes security, protection, comfort, and approval—vitally important commodities, in their minds. When a husband shows his wife affection, he sends the following messages:

"I'll take care of you and protect you. You are important to me, and I don't want anything to happen to you."

"I'm concerned about the problems you face, and I am with you."

"I think you've done a good job, and I'm proud of you."

A hug can say any one or all of the above. Men need to understand how strongly women need these affirmations. For the *typical wife*, daily affirmation goes a long way. Hugging is a skill most men need to develop to show their wives affection. It is also a simple but effective way to build the connection between a wife and husband.[23]

Most women love to hug. They hug each other; they hug children, animals, relatives—even stuffed animals. In most cases, a hug will produce a very positive response. There are other ways of showing affection that can be effective for a woman. A greeting card or note expressing love and care simply but effectively communicates the same emotions. Don't forget that all-time-favorite: flowers. Women, almost universally, love to receive flowers. Occasionally, you can find a man who likes to receive them, but most do not. For most women, however, flowers send a powerful message of love or concern. An invitation to dinner also shows affection. It is a way of saying to one's wife, "You need a break today, so I want to take you out for dinner."

Jokes abound on how, almost immediately after the wedding, a wife has to open her own car door, open the door at home, and find her own chair at restaurants. A sensitive husband will open a

---

[23] Ed Young, *Romancing the Home* (Broadman and Holman Publishers, Nashville, Tennessee, 1993), p. 83.

door for her at every opportunity—it is another way to tell her, "I love you and cherish you." Holding hands is a time-honored and effective sign of affection. Walks after dinner, back rubs, phone calls, and conversations with thoughtful and loving expressions all add up in her mind. As more than one song has expressed, "There are a thousand ways to say 'I love you.'" From a woman's point of view, affection is the essential cement in her relationship with a man. Without it, a woman most probably feels alienated from her mate. With it, she feels a tight bond to him. Some men will say, "But she knows I'm not the affectionate type." Men must get into their heads this vital idea: women find affection important in its own right. They love the feeling that accompanies both the giving and receiving of affection, but it has nothing to do with sex. Most of the affection they give and receive is not intended to be sexual.[24]

All of this confuses the typical male. Seemingly, showing affection for him is part of sexual foreplay, and he is normally aroused in a flash. In other cases, men simply want to skip the affection business and get right to the sexual part.

If you want the "one flesh" experience to be all that it was intended to be, remember this: "When it comes to sex and affection, you can't have one without the other!"[25]

Wives who feel increasingly frustrated about non-responsive husbands will dwell on their frustration until they come up with a theory that they think fits their situation. Unresponsive husbands will totally frustrate their wives. As a result, women will attempt a number of different approaches in order to bring life back into their marriage. And also as a result, their husbands will become totally confused over what is taking place in their homes.[26] The wife may simply back off and separate herself from the rest of

[24] Willard F. Harley Jr., *His Needs Her Needs* (Fleming H. Revell, a division of Baker Books, 1992), p. 73.

[25] Ibid., p.

[26] Ken Nair, *Discovering the Mind of a Woman* (Thomas Nelson, Nashville, 1995), p. 132.

the family, becoming passive in her routine, not showing any joy or excitement. This whole process will simply compound the woman's guilty feelings of low self-worth that she has already been experiencing due to her husband's lack of interest in her. She knows that giving up is not the answer, but she gets totally worn out by the struggle to figure things out and change them.[27]

One of the strongest desires of a wife is to know that her husband needs her. With an unresponsive husband, the woman recognizes that her husband is indifferent, and that is the same as personal rejection.[28] It is not unusual for a wife to want her husband to be attentive and appreciate her as a person and to show her that he needs her.

All of this comes back to what God intended for the wife to be: a helper suitable for her husband. So when the wife feels she is not needed, her whole purpose in creation is brought into consideration. She may falsely conclude, "If he doesn't need me, why should I stay here?"

The man needs to understand that he has a responsibility to the woman to help her fulfill her God-given responsibility. This is part of the command of 1 Peter 3:7, where Peter tells husbands, "Dwell with them [wives] according to knowledge." Women are different from men and require specific understanding if men are going to enjoy what God intended to bless them with—helpers suitable for them. Most men are simply confused by women, and this confusion is apparent in the world we live in. I believe that is why Peter brought this whole subject up for men to hear and act upon.

Learning to solve relationship problems is critical for the well-being of every family. Unsolved problems in the home, especially those between the husband and the wife, will frustrate a husband. Any ongoing frustrations will destroy his endurance,

---

[27] Ibid., p. 131.
[28] Ibid., p. 133.

eventually resulting in the husband losing interest in the marriage and backing away from caring for his wife.[29] It is not the actual problem that wears a man down; it is his inability to solve the problem that creates the mess.

We read in Judges 21:25 that there was a time when men were left alone and the result was, "everyone did what was right in his own eyes." That really is the way natural men react to everything. We find Solomon writing in Proverbs about the contrast between the human and the divine perspectives: "Every way of a man is right in his own eyes, but the LORD weighs the hearts" (Judges 21:2). God is placing a strong emphasis on the heart. He does not merely notice what is obvious to the eyes. He looks at the more important matters, the emotions, the feelings of the heart, where women tend to spend a lot of time. Proverbs 16:2 highlights God's ability to judge the spirit: "All the ways of a man are pure in his own eyes, but the LORD weighs the spirits."

---

[29] Ibid., p. 107.

CHAPTER 4

God's Diversity

Personality Traits

Your personal temperament influences everything you do. You are not the temperament you are because you do certain things. Rather, you act the way you do because of your temperament. There are very few things in your life that are not influenced by your temperament. We need to learn about our temperaments in order to discover our strengths and weaknesses. Humanly speaking, there is nothing that impacts your life as much as your temperament or combination of temperaments. That is the reason it is so important to know your temperament and to be willing to look at other people's temperaments with an eye to see what they are and what you can assume. With God's help, we can overcome our weaknesses and take advantage of our strengths.

Temperament is passed on through the genes and no doubt has been affected by Adam's sin. Paul expressed this point very well in Romans 7:18–20:

> For to will is present with me; but how to perform that which is good I find not. For the good that

I would I do not; but the evil which I would not, that I do. Now if I do that I would not, it is no more I that do it, but sin that dwelleth in me.

Paul made a distinction between himself and that uncontrollable force that was fighting from within. The "I" is Paul's person—the soul, will, and mind of man. The "sin" that dwelled in him was the human nature that all of us have.[30]

Temperament, Character, and Personality

Temperament is the combination of traits that subconsciously affect a person's behavior. These traits are arranged genetically on the basis of nationality, race, sex, and other hereditary factors. No one knows where in the body it takes residence, probably somewhere in the brain or emotional center (often referred to as the heart).[31]

It is a person's temperament that determines whether a person is an introvert or extrovert. Looking at a particular family with multiple children, you will see that each child will have his or her own particular behavior. The environment does not create it, but does tend to encourage what is already present in the individual. Brothers and sisters can be, and usually are, very different in their makeup, all due to a difference in their temperament. The home life can influence a person, as well as training, discipline, and education, but temperament is the primary influence on a person's life.[32]

Extroverts may tone down their outgoing behavior, but they will never change it; they will always be extroverts. Likewise,

---

[30] Tim LaHaye, *Why You Act the Way You Do* (Tyndale House, Wheaton, Illinois, 1984), p. 20.
[31] Ibid., p. 21.
[32] Ibid., p. 23.

introverts will never become extroverts; they may work at being more outgoing but will never change their basic behavior. Temperament sets broad guidelines on everyone's behavior; these patterns will influence a person as long as he or she lives.

This basic nature that we have all inherited from our parents is called several things in the Bible: "the natural man," "the flesh," "the old man," and "corruptible flesh," plus others. This provides the impulses of our being as we try to meet the needs of life. It is very important to distinguish between temperament, character, and personality.

Temperament

Temperament is the combination of traits received at birth that subconsciously affect a person's behavior. These traits are arranged genetically on the basis of nationality, race, sex, and other hereditary factors.[33] These traits are passed on through the genes. Some psychologists believe that the majority of our genes come from the grandparents. Sometimes, the resemblance to grandparents is remarkable, even astounding. However, there is no way to predict the alignment of traits in an individual based on the parents or grandparents.

Character

Character is the real you. The Bible calls it "the hidden man of the heart." It is the result of your natural temperament modified by childhood training, education, basic attitudes, beliefs, principles, and motivations. It is sometimes referred to as the soul of an individual, which is made up of the mind, emotions, and will.

---

[33] Ibid., p. 23.

Personality

Personality is the outward expression of ourselves, which may or may not be the same as our character, depending on how genuine we are. Bringing these all together, we see that temperament is the combination of traits we were born with; character is our "civilized" temperament; and personality is the face we show others.

Many people go through life acting a part on the basis of what they think they should be; they have a particular way they want others to view them. This results in a false public persona that really hides the individual from most people. This is one reason for mental and spiritual chaos in the lives of many people.[34]

Temperament traits, whether controlled or uncontrolled, last throughout our life. The older we get, the softer our harsh and hard traits tend to become.

The Foundation

The heart of the temperament theory, as first conceived by Hippocrates over twenty-four hundred years ago, divides people into four basic categories, which he named sanguine, choleric, melancholy, and phlegmatic. Each temperament has both strengths and weaknesses that form a distinct part of one's makeup throughout life.[35] The Bible says that "Man looks on the outward appearance, but God looks on the heart" and "Out of the heart proceeds the issues of life." Change needs to start on the inside of an individual if real change is going to take place at all.

So temperament is the combination of traits we were all born with, character is our presentation to others, and personality is the face we show to others. Understand that temperament traits come

---

[34] Ibid., p. 24.
[35] Tim LaHaye, *Why Your Act the Way You Act* (Tyndale House, Wheaton, Illinois, 1984), p. 11.

genetically from our parents but are not predictable. Traits can be influenced by nationality, race, and temperament. A person's sex will also affect temperament, especially in relation to emotions. Women can be more expressive emotionally than men. The most controlled and hardened women will weep at times, but some men never weep, regardless of the situation.

Temperament traits will last your entire life, regardless of how much effort is put into controlling or even changing them. It seems that the older one gets, the mellower one's harsh traits become. Most people learn that emphasizing their strengths and controlling their weaknesses helps them get through life easier. Many people are successful at realizing their strengths and developing them, which builds character and improves their personality. No one can change his or her temperament, but it is possible to recognize your strengths and weaknesses and respond accordingly. It is possible to work on your temperament traits in such a way as to appear entirely different for a while, but ultimately you will revert back to your real self when left alone.[36]

Your Temperament

There are four basic temperaments, and each has positive and negative aspects. Hippocrates saw people consistently fall into four categories, which he named sanguine, choleric, melancholy, and phlegmatic. Learning one's temperament actually enables a person to make better choices as to work, activities, and friendships.

The first temperament is called sanguine. The sanguine is a warm, buoyant, lively, and "enjoying" person who is receptive by nature. External impressions easily find their way to the sanguine's heart, where they cause an outburst of response. Sanguines have an unusual capacity for enjoying themselves and passing on their fun-loving spirit. The moment this person enters a room, everyone

---

[36] Ibid., p. 27.

has their spirits lifted. They never lack for friends. People often excuse their wrong behavior because they are so likeable.

The apostle Peter in the Bible could be labeled a sanguine. Every time he appears in the gospels, he has something to say; he dominates the group and generally is very vocal. As you read through the gospels, you will find that Peter talked more than all the other disciples combined. That is very typical for a sanguine temperament. The sanguine often will speak before thinking or weighing the words that are about to come out. Early in Peter's account, we find that to be very common.

Later in life, Peter was able to get a handle on his tendencies to speak before thinking. People look at sanguines and usually feel good when they are present. This feel-good attitude on the part of others can be seen in their reluctance to condemn shortcomings, instead saying, "That's just the way he is."[37]

The second temperament is the choleric. This temperament is hot, quick, active, practical, strong-willed, self-sufficient, and very independent. He tends to be very decisive and opinionated, finding it easy to make decisions both for himself and other people. Like the sanguine, the choleric is an extrovert, but is not nearly so intense. Mr. Choleric thrives on activity. He does not need to be stimulated by his environment, but rather stimulates his environment with his endless ideas, plans, goals, and ambitions. He does not engage in aimless activity, for he has a practical, keen mind, capable of making sound, instant decisions or planning worthwhile projects. He does not bend under pressure from others, but takes a definite stand on issues. His dogged determination usually allows him to succeed where others have failed.[38]

Mr. Choleric's emotional nature is the least developed part of his temperament. He does not sympathize easily with others,

---

[37] Ibid., p. 27.
[38] Ibid., p. 28.

nor does he naturally show or express compassion. Not given to analysis, but rather to quick, almost intuitive appraisal, the choleric tends to look at the goal without seeing the pitfalls along the way. He tends to be domineering and bossy and does not hesitate to use people. Once he has decided on a project, he may simply run headlong into the work, stepping on people as he goes. Sometimes people will look at this person as an opportunist.

The third temperament is the melancholy. This temperament is the richest of all the temperaments. They are analytical, self-sacrificing, gifted, perfectionist types with a very sensitive emotional nature. No one gets more enjoyment from the fine arts than the melancholy. By nature, they are prone to be introverts; but since their feelings predominate, they are given to a variety of moods. Sometimes those moods will lift them to heights of ecstasy that cause them to act more extroverted. However, at other times, they will be gloomy and depressed, and during these periods, they become withdrawn and can be quite antagonistic.[39]

The melancholy is a very faithful friend but, unlike the sanguine, does not make friends easily. They seldom push themselves forward to meet people; rather, they wait for people to come to them. They are perhaps the most dependable of all the temperaments, for their perfectionistic and conscientious tendencies do not permit them to be shirkers or let others down who are counting on them. Disappointing experiences make them reluctant to take people at face value; thus, they are prone to be suspicious when others seek them out or shower them with praise.

Their exceptional analytical ability causes them to diagnose accurately the obstacles and dangers of any project they have a part in planning. This is in sharp contrast to the choleric, who rarely anticipates problems or difficulties, but is confident of being able to cope with whatever crises may arise. Occasionally, a mood of emotional ecstasy or inspiration will produce some great work of

---

[39] Ibid., p. 29.

art or genius. But these accomplishments are often followed by periods of great depression.

The Melancholy usually finds greatest meaning in life through personal sacrifice. They seem desirous of making themselves suffer, and they will often choose a difficult vocation involving great personal sacrifice. But once it is chosen, they are prone to be very thorough and persistent in their pursuit of it. They more than likely will accomplish some great good if the natural tendency to gripe throughout the sacrificial process doesn't get them so depressed that they give up on it altogether. No temperament has so much natural potential when energized by the Holy Spirit as the melancholy.[40]

The phlegmatic is the fourth temperament. Phlegmatics are the calm, easygoing, never-get-upset individuals with such a high boiling point that they almost never become angry. They are the easiest type of person to get along with and are by nature the most likable of all the temperaments. The name *phlegmatic* is derived from what Hippocrates thought was the body fluid that produced the "calm, cool, slow, well-balanced temperament." Life for them is a happy, unexcited, pleasant experience in which they avoid as much involvement as possible. They are so calm and unruffled that they never seem agitated, no matter what circumstances surround them. They are of the one temperament type that is consistent every time you see them. Beneath his cool, almost timid personality, Mr. Phlegmatic has a very capable combination of abilities. He feels more emotion than what appears on the surface and appreciates the fine arts and the beautiful things of life. Usually, he avoids violence.

Phlegmatics do not lack for friends because they enjoy people and have a natural dry sense of humor. They are the types who can have a crowd of people in stitches, yet never crack a smile.

Most phlegmatics tend to be spectators in life and try not

---

[40] Ibid., p. 29.

to get very involved with the activities of others. In fact, it is usually with great reluctance that they are ever motivated to any form of activity beyond their daily routine. This does not mean, however, that they cannot appreciate the need for action and the predicaments of others. A phlegmatic and a choleric may confront the same social injustice, but their responses will be entirely different. The choleric would probably say, "Let's organize and campaign to do something about this!" The phlegmatic would likely respond, "These conditions are terrible! Why doesn't someone do something about them?" Usually, the very kindhearted and sympathetic phlegmatics seldom convey their true feelings. When once aroused to action, however, their capable, efficient qualities become apparent. They will not volunteer to leadership on their own, but when it is forced on them, they prove to be very capable leaders. They have a conciliating effect on others and are natural peacemakers.[41]

Your Response to Temperament Strengths

It is very easy to get discouraged when looking at our temperaments, but there is help. In Romans 8:37, we read, "we are more than conquerors through him [Jesus Christ] that loved us." God can deal with our weaknesses when we allow the Holy Spirit to take charge. The key is to understand what our weaknesses are so we can prayerfully deal with them. It is the same with our strengths.

The Sanguine

The strengths of the sanguine: they are not just extroverts, but super-extroverts. Everything they do is superficial and external. They laugh loudly and dominate every conversation, whether they have anything to say or not. They love the limelight and are very

---

[41] Ibid., p. 30.

good at public speaking. They generally will start a conversation, not willing to wait for another person to start it.

Sanguines have the ability to respond instantly to others. If they see another person looking their way, they always respond with a nod, wink or greeting. No one is more sociable. And they never lose their curiosity of things. If they don't like something, all they have to do is change their surroundings. Going to a different room or location is all that is needed to get their minds off of what they did not like. It is very seldom that sanguines wake up in a bad mood. They will whistle or sing their way through life.[42]

Here is the strength of the sanguine: They have the God-given ability to live in the present. They easily forget the past and are seldom frustrated or fearful of future difficulties. They are always optimistic and can inspire others, often carrying them along on some new venture.

If yesterday's project failed, they are confident that today's will succeed. Sanguines absolutely love people and must be around them and with them whenever possible.

Nobody makes a better first impression.

Summary: Sanguines have tender, compassionate hearts. No one responds more genuinely to the needs of others than the sanguine. They are able to share the emotional experiences, both good and bad, of others. By nature, they find it easy to obey the scriptural command to "Rejoice with those that do rejoice, and weep with those who weep." Others often misunderstand the sincerity of sanguines. They are deceived by their sudden changes of emotion and they fail to understand that they are genuinely responding to the emotions of others. No one can love you more or forget you faster than a sanguine. The world is better off for having these people involved and active. When under the control of the Holy Spirit, they can be great servants of Jesus Christ.

---

[42] Ibid., p. 26.

The Choleric

Strengths: Cholerics are usually self-disciplined individuals with a strong tendency toward self-determination. They are very confident in their own ability and very aggressive. They can appear to be overbearing and insensitive, which often keeps people at a distance.

Cholerics are very determined people who, once having started a project, have a strong will that keeps them pushing ahead; stubbornness is often what is projected. This stubbornness can be an asset when the going gets difficult, but going on is an absolute necessity for any choleric.[43] This results in many projects being completed that might otherwise be dropped by other people.

The Choleric temperament is oriented almost entirely toward the practical aspects of life. Everything is looked at in relation to its practical purpose. They really are relaxed when involved with some worthwhile project; sometimes it just needs to be an activity of any kind to keep them happy. They can be very organized but finds the details annoying; organizing is often done when the project is finished or in between jobs. Most of their decisions are reached more by intuition than by analytical reasoning; their gut feelings are very important and often are the way they deal with many decisions. When asked why they decided something, their responses will often have no real factual basis.

Cholerics have strong leadership abilities. Their forceful will often dominates a group; they find it difficult to sit back and let others dominant the group. They are good judges of character, and they are quick and aggressive in emergencies. Not only will they accept leadership when it is offered to them, but they will often ask for it.

If they can control their aggressiveness, others will respond well to their leadership. If people do not agree with them, that

---

[43] Ibid., p. 30.

doesn't really bother them. It does not intimidate them at all to stand alone or be the only dissenter. Cholerics can and will go against the tide, resist the crowd, and stand alone. It really doesn't bother them to be the only one on any issue. They certainly are not swayed by the majority or pressure from the crowd.

Summary: No one is more practical than a choleric. They seem to have a practical mentality. They have strong workaholic tendencies that can intimidate those around them. Fellow workers often resent the fact that they will do more, do it longer, and do it better than the rest. Cholerics' outlook on life, based on their natural feeling of self-confidence, is almost always one of optimism. They have such a go-getter spirit that they think nothing of leaving a secure position for the challenge of the unknown; it is nothing to leave behind a job for the possibility of something unproven. Adversity does not discourage them. Instead, it increases their appetite and makes them ever more determined to achieve their goals.[44]

The Melancholy

Strengths: Usually, melancholies have the highest IQ of anyone in their family. They may be musical, artistic, or athletic; often all of these traits will be present with the melancholy. They have a very sensitive nature: more geniuses are melancholy than any other type. They will excel in the fine arts; cultural things are very important to them, and these individuals are very responsive, but their emotions will create some deep thoughts that often drive them into deep depression.

Melancholies can achieve some very creative thinking, which can produce some great responses. These people tend to be perfectionists; they have a very high standard that tends to exceed that of other people. Acceptability is very important to the melancholy and must be maintained at all costs.

---

[44] Ibid., p. 28.

Their analytical abilities, combined with their perfectionist tendencies, make him sticklers for detail. This can drive other people crazy and impact their acceptability by others. With any new project, they can analyze it in a few minutes and find every potential problem. These people are very dependable; you can always count on them to finish their jobs and do them on time.

They do not seek out attention and prefer to work behind the scenes. There is a strong desire to do something for the betterment of humankind. They tend to be reserved and seldom volunteer their opinions or ideas. Melancholy individuals are usually very self-disciplined people.

Summary: They rarely eat too much or indulge their own comforts. When they engage in a task, they will work around the clock to meet deadlines and their high self-imposed standards. One of the reasons they can go into a deep depression after completion of a big project is because they have so neglected themselves while completing the project by going without sleep, food, and diversion that they are literally exhausted, physically and emotionally.

The Phlegmatic

Strengths: Just because they are super-introverts does not mean phlegmatics are not strong. Their calm and cool nature is a vital asset. In emergencies, they can stay very calm. There are things they can do and vocations they can pursue that extroverts could never do. They rarely, if ever, leap before they look. They are thinkers and planners.

Phlegmatics are conciliatory by nature; they do not like confrontation and would rather negotiate than fight. They have a way of defusing hostile and excitable people. They are walking examples that "a soft answer turns away wrath."

Phlegmatics never get very involved; this gives them the ability to see the humor in almost any situation. Their timing is what makes their comments humorous. They can be very stimulating in conversation because of their imagination. A phlegmatic is Mr. Dependability. Not only can he be depended upon to always be his cheerful, good-natured self, but he can be depended on to fulfill his obligations and time schedules. This trait makes them very faithful friends, though they rarely get involved with others.

They are practical and efficient, not given to making sudden decisions. They have a way of finding the practical way to do something with the least amount of effort. He can do their best work under conditions that would be totally unacceptable to others. Their work areas are always neat and clean. Though they are not perfectionists, they do have exceptionally high standards of accuracy and precision.

Summary: The administrative or leadership abilities of a phlegmatic are seldom discovered because they are not assertive and don't push, but when once given the responsibility, they have a real ability to get people to work together productively and in an organized manner.[45]

Note: The different temperaments keep the world functioning. No one individual temperament is more desirable than another. Each one has its vital strengths and makes its worthwhile contribution to life. Someone once said, "The hard-driving choleric produces the inventions of the genius-prone melancholy, which are sold by the personable sanguine and enjoyed by the easygoing phlegmatic."[46]

Your Responses to Temperament Weaknesses

No one likes to be confronted with their weaknesses. But if we think of ourselves only in terms of the strengths of our temperaments,

---

[45] Ibid., p. 30.
[46] Ibid., p. 33.

we will develop a false view of ourselves. Remember, everyone has some weaknesses.

The sanguine weaknesses: A sanguine is very often voted "most likely to succeed"; unfortunately, they often are the first to fail in life. Their tendency to be weak-willed and undisciplined will finally destroy them unless it is overcome. Since they are very emotional, have a lot of natural charm, and are prone to be what one psychologist called "touchers" (that is, they tend to touch people as they talk to them), they often have a great appeal for the opposite sex and consequently face sexual temptation more than others.

Weakness of will and lack of discipline make it easier for them to be deceitful, dishonest, and undependable. Sanguines have the ability to overdo; they tend to overeat and gain weight. They find it hard to remain on a diet. Someone has said, "Without self-discipline, there is no such thing as success." Lack of discipline is the biggest problem for a sanguine.

Sanguines have very strong emotions. The only temperament more emotional than a sanguine is a melancholy. Not only can sanguines cry at the drop of a hat, but their anger can be set off instantly. Lack of emotional consistency usually limits them vocationally, and it certainly destroys them spiritually. When filled with the Spirit, however, they become a "new creature," an emotionally controlled sanguine.

Sanguines are generally very disorganized and always on the move. They seldom plan ahead, but usually take things as they come. They rarely profit by past mistakes and seldom look ahead for pitfalls. They tend to be disorganized, accidents waiting to happen. Their homes are in a disorganized state; they can never find their tools, even though they are right where they left them.[47] The sanguine garage, bedroom, closet, and office are disaster areas unless they have efficient wives and secretaries willing to

---

[47] Ibid., p. 34.

pick up after them. Their egotism usually makes them sharp dressers, but if their friends or customers could see the room where they dressed, they would think that a tornado had just swept through the room.

They get away with all of this with a big smile, a pat on the back, a joke or two, and a fast change of direction to the next thing that attracts their interest. The sanguine will never be a perfectionist.

The Spirit of God can bring some order and discipline into these people's lives.

When this happens, they are much happier people, not only with others, but also with themselves. When the Spirit is in control, sanguines are outstanding people. Sanguines will often have a false reputation of self-confidence, but they can be very unstable in their own minds.

Sanguines are very bold and not mindful of getting hurt. This often results in wild feats of heroism. However, they are fearful of personal failure, rejection, or disapproval. These are the individuals that will go along with the crowd, rather than face disapproval; they will try to cover up a problem with something else that you will approve of to distract you.

Sanguines have shaky consciences. Perhaps the most difficult trait for sanguines is their bending, movable conscience. They usually are able to talk others into their way of thinking. This results in them being viewed as con artists, not always trustworthy. Whenever things go wrong, they are quick to justify their actions and refuse to accept responsibility for the problem. They are very good at modifying the truth until any similarity between their account and the actual event is totally accidental, yet they seldom get convicted over this. Not only can they deceive others, but they actually can believe their own stories because the end justifies the means. The only way to deal with this is to focus on the facts and honesty. Every time we lie or cheat, the next time becomes easier.

Sanguines have a tendency for describing things much bigger, better, and easier than they really are. While they can maintain their deception to those who seldom see them, it is impossible for them to do these things without teaching their spouses and children that they cannot depend on the sanguines' words. One of the main ingredients in marriage is trust; this is what a lasting marriage is built upon. It is critical for sanguines to learn to discipline themselves and control their weak tendencies in order for their families to trust them.[48]

The choleric weaknesses: Cholerics are extremely confrontational people. Some learn to control their anger, but sudden violence is constantly a possibility with them. If their strong will is not brought under control by proper parental discipline as children, they develop angry, tumultuous habits that follow them throughout life. Proverbs 22:6 is especially needed with this individual early in life: "Train up a child in the way that he should go: and when he is old, he will not depart from it."

It does not take them long to learn that they can intimidate others with their angry outbursts and that they can use wrath as a means to get what they want. This temperament can easily cause pain to others, and they can actually enjoy doing it. They usually have very strained relationships with their spouses, and the children are either afraid or filled with anger themselves. A choleric's child often is the neighborhood bully, imitating what he or she sees from his parent.

Cholerics are volcanoes waiting for an eruption. They love a fight and almost seem to get energized by one. They tend to always be on the edge of exploding at someone or something. They are door slammers, table pounders, and horn blowers. Anyone that gets in their way will feel their full wrath.

Cholerics can be very sharp with their language. No one delivers more hurtful comments. They always are ready and willing to destroy weaker temperaments. Even though sanguines are very

---

[48] Ibid., p. 71.

good at overpowering people with their constant conversation, they cannot stand up to cholerics. A sanguine can have a lot to say at the drop of a hat, but the sanguine is generally not a cruel person. A choleric will stomp on you in a flash and think nothing of it.

Cholerics can leave a number of people hurting and wondering what just happened to them. While cholerics can wipe out others, in the process they destroy any sense of personal joy that could have been theirs.

There is not a more noticeable temperament difference than when the Holy Spirit gets control of a choleric's tongue. When cholerics learn the impact of their verbal approval and encouragement to others, they will try to get a handle on their hostility—until they get angry, and then they discover what the apostle James meant when he said, "the tongue can no man tame; it is an unruly evil, full of deadly poison" (James 3:8).

The quick response to others, along with an angry spirit, often combine to make a choleric very profane. The choleric is the least sympathetic of all the temperaments.

The idea of kindness is often strange to them. They are the most unaffectionate of all the temperaments and have a very difficult time showing any public emotion.

Being married to a choleric is difficult when it comes to affection. Because of their overpowering temperament, it is difficult for cholerics to show tenderness and compassion. Marital affection to them is a real problem; they do not respond well to it and have difficulty expressing it.

Rarely will you see a choleric cry; they usually stop around the age of eleven or twelve. Along with their lack of affection is their insensitive response to the needs of others. When they are sensitive and considerate, they can be a benefit to others. Cholerics usually possess a thick skin and can take a lot of abuse. The Spirit of God can transform this temperament to be kind and tenderhearted.

Cholerics can dig their heels in quickly and at the same time have advice for anyone and everyone, regardless of whether they wanted it or not. Like every temperament, their strengths can become problems when not controlled. Since they have an intuitive sense, they can make up their minds quickly when dealing with any matter (they do not care about analysis and deliberation), and once they have made a decision, that is it—no going back, no changing. No temperament cares as little about the facts as this one: "Don't confuse me with the facts; my mind is made up." However, cholerics can be very effective because of their unbending, never-say-die attitude. If their weaknesses are not allowed to control them, cholerics can accomplish a lot.

When they are filled with the Holy Spirit, their tendencies toward willfulness and harshness are replaced by a gentleness which shows clearly that they are controlled by something other than their own natural temperament.[49]

The melancholy weaknesses: There are times when perfection and conscientiousness are very important, but when these attributes are dominant, they often present problems. Melancholies can be extremely negative and pessimistic and show a tendency to criticize. Anyone who has ever worked with a melancholy knows that they tend to be negative about everything until they get additional information. This often limits melancholies where they work. Anytime a new project is presented, a melancholy immediately sees all the problems and all the ways the project can fail. Others find it hard to be around this person; they restrict the interaction among workers. People will find reasons to keep their distance from melancholies and avoid asking for an opinion on anything. This one trait makes promotion and any type of advancement difficult, unless the boss is a choleric who is able to see past the immediate negativity.

The most damaging influence upon a person's mind is

---

[49] Ibid., p. 73

criticism, and melancholies have to deal with that constantly. Most disturbed children come from homes with choleric or melancholy parents: the choleric parent terrorizes the children, but melancholy parents destroy them with criticism.

Even when melancholies think they should praise their wives or husbands, they struggle. It is hard because they choke trying to say something that is not 100 percent correct. This same trait will make melancholies totally unable to give themselves any credit.

Melancholies have a tendency to do themselves in. Self-examination is needed by all of us, but a melancholy will go to an extreme. Melancholies will be their own worst critics, dissecting every single action until they have nothing left to hang onto. Their self-confidence and self-esteem are the first to go. Melancholies constantly look at others and then compare themselves, always falling short, never considering that they are looking at everyone else's most favorable traits and not their weaknesses. Even on a spiritual level, melancholies see themselves as not measuring up to God's standards and struggle with the idea that God can accept them as they are. Melancholies find it difficult to believe they are "approved of God," basically because they can seldom approve themselves.

Melancholies tend to be extremely sensitive; every word, every action by others is seen as judgment, criticism, or rejection. Their self-centered trait, together with their sensitive nature, makes melancholies thin-skinned and touchy at times.

Melancholies are not as explosive as sanguines or cholerics, but still they can produce some potent fire, seething with revengeful thinking. Melancholies who do not learn to control their thought patterns can easily turn into manic-depressives.[50]

One of the main characteristics of melancholies is the ability to change moods very quickly and dramatically. On one day, they are on top of the world and can be mistaken for sanguines;

---

[50] Ibid., p. 74.

on another occasion, they are in the valley of depression, and nothing you say can help. The older they get, the more severe the depression becomes, unless energized by the Holy Spirit. When they get into one of their moods, it is impossible to please them, opening the door for deep depression.

Melancholies need to meditate on 1 Thessalonians 5:18: "In everything give thanks for this is the will of God in Christ Jesus concerning you." You cannot give thanks and stay in a state of depression. God knows what He is doing. Melancholies are unbending. No other temperament is so easily given to solidly unbending positions. Melancholies can be intolerant and impatient with other points of view. This makes them often very lonely and not able to work well on a team. At home, the rest of the family can be made to feel very insecure and unhappy and sometimes write them off altogether. They need to learn how to compromise and to be more flexible. If things are not done their way, a mood swing is inevitable. They need to relax and understand it is not the end of the world when things are not done exactly as they think they should be done.

Melancholies are generally idealists. This tendency makes them pursue impractical goals or things that will never work out in the end. To be successful, they must look at their situation from a practical standpoint and evaluate it in light of realistic possibilities. The Holy Spirit needs full control of these individuals.

The phlegmatic weaknesses: A phlegmatic temperament is never in a rush for anything. *Phleg* means slow or sluggish. Although phlegmatics do everything expected of them, they will never, or at least rarely, do more than expected. They see involvement with others as something to stay away from; involvement means responsibility. These people will gravitate toward nothing; they are very content to do nothing. They will seldom be seen starting a new project.

Phlegmatics are sensitive about everything, yet they often refuse to show their feelings to others. No one likes to be hurt, and they are no exception. They are not as sensitive as melancholies, but are easily hurt by others. That is one reason they do not get involved—because that takes away the possibility of getting hurt by something someone may say to them or about them.

Phlegmatics will often think of disappearing, just finding an out-of-the-way place to crawl into when they are facing criticism or confrontation. Nothing gets done unless they learn to bear the burden of some criticism. They also need to realize that dealing with other people means they will get hurt on occasion.

Phlegmatics can show a real selfish streak. This trait does not appear readily but can become a problem for a phlegmatic. Every temperament has this problem, but none as severe as a phlegmatic. Only those people who live with them would know that this problem even exists.

Phlegmatics can be very self-indulgent and show no interest in the needs of their families. No one can be more stubborn, but they are so diplomatic that it often does not come across that way. They may actually seem to agree with others and then simply do what they want. With no actual confrontation, this type of action can be very frustrating for others. At home, phlegmatics will not argue with their spouses; they just will not do it, whatever the *it* is.

Phlegmatics suffer from all types of fear. They are worriers by nature; this shows up constantly in decision-making or the lack thereof. They need to read Philippians 4:6 and believe it: "Be anxious for nothing." This fear will often keep them from trying something new. This same fear keeps them from serving in the church because they are afraid of failure or criticism. One of the strengths of the Holy Spirit is faith which takes away our fear: "For God has not given us the spirit of fear" (1 Timothy 1:7). Every phlegmatic needs to read this verse on a daily basis. Once committed, phlegmatics respond very well.[51]

This is not the point to give up in frustration over our

---

[51] Ibid., p. 74.

temperamental weaknesses. The Lord can and will overcome them to equip you to become what you should be. We need to read the Word of God and believe every word. God cannot and will not lie!

Male Characteristics

While the temperaments are certainly a major part of every person, there are still distinct differences between men and women above and apart from temperaments. These differences can be viewed as male and female characteristics. These characteristics are, however, impacted by the individual temperaments. Men and women are totally unique and different from each other. Even though a couple may have the same temperament, they will still possess unique qualities that are the result of their gender. A husband and wife may work at the same job, but they will in most cases have very different outlooks concerning their work. Prior to their marriage, the differences may have attracted each to the other, but in marriage, these same traits can be viewed as threats.[52]

These differences begin with the physical aspects of each; the male is physically stronger than the female. This goes along with God's plan for men to be the protectors of women. History has shown a pattern of dependence upon men for protection and what men by their strength can provide.

As we continue, we see from the creation account that the responsibility of managing the earth's resources was part of God's plan for Adam. In Genesis 2:15, we read, "Then the Lord God took the man and put him into the Garden of Eden, to cultivate it and to keep it." As a result, men generally show a desire to be the ones who provides for their families. It is not a role they develop, but one that is innate; it is the very nature of their masculinity.

---

[52] James Walker, *Husbands Who Won't Lead and Wives Who Won't Follow* (Bethany House Publishers, Minnesota, 2000), p. 13.

Men find a great deal of satisfaction from their labor, to the extent that women may feel they are in competition with men's work.

A woman is made physically, emotionally, and spiritually for the main purpose of nurturing. Genesis 2:18: "And the Lord God said it is not good that the man should be alone; I will make him a help meet for him." The female nature is one of responding and receiving. The basic nature of a woman is to respond to the leadership of her husband.[53] This is evident in the way men and women listen to a conversation. A woman hears emotionally; men tend to hear only the facts. Many a woman has married a man who loves the Lord but has no idea how to love her. This is the result of failing to understand how God made them and how He intended them to work and live together. We read in 1 Peter 3:7 this command: "Likewise, you husbands, dwell with them [wives] according to knowledge, giving honor unto the wife, as unto the weaker vessel, and as being heirs together of the grace of life; that your prayers be not hindered." Here is a direct command from God for men to learn to understand their wives, who are obviously different.

The biblical role of a man does not stop when he comes home from work. Many men simply see their responsibility to provide for the family as their sole obligation. The ability to provide material things for the family is not the sum total of his responsibility. Paul gave Timothy a list of qualifications for any man who would be an "overseer" in the church: "He must be one who manages his own household well, keeping his children under control with all dignity (but if a man does not know how to manage his own household, how will he take care of the church of God?)" (1 Timothy 3:4–5).

The role of manager applies to every man. His job is not finished when he comes home. The management of his home should be a top priority. While many women now contribute to

---

[53] Ibid., p. 14.

the financial needs of the family, the home is still considered to be the women's responsibility. Over the past decade, *USA Today* surveyed more than 100,000 people in over 100 public opinion polls. The results are very telling. They write:

> Consider this: In this age of liberation and equal opportunity, 94 percent of all women who live with a man say they do more work around the home. And the men agree. Surprisingly, however, only about 1 in 5 women—21 percent—wish the men would do more around the house. This is the key to understanding the conflict for women ... As they expand their horizons, they are not all sure they want to give up the thing that has always given them self-esteem—the ability to take care of their home and family.[54]

Men desperately need to understand what women think and what moves them. Most men cannot agree on very much, but one thing they do agree on is the idea that women are a pure mystery. In fact, many men having been raised with the idea that women are a mystery, so they make no attempt to understand the women in their lives. This is not unique to America; it can be seen around the world. But this simply underscores the fact that men and women are different. The apostle Peter, having written that men should live with their wives in an understanding way, gave men encouragement that it was possible to understand women.

A major obstacle for men in understanding women is their belief that the problem lies

---

[54] Ibid., p. 176.

with the women. If only women would think differently, act differently, or respond differently, everything would be fine. Because a woman is a responder, she is simply doing what she does in response to her husband's actions. Men rarely make the connection between their actions and women's reactions. The Bible clearly makes men responsible, not only for their own actions, but also for the condition of their marriages.[55]

If we take a serious look at Genesis 3:6, we will find that God held Adam accountable for the first sin by refusing to protect his wife from making a terrible mistake in judgment. The verse reads, "And when the woman saw that the tree was good for food, and that it was pleasant to the eyes, and a tree to be desired to make one wise, she took of the fruit thereof, and did eat, and gave also unto her husband with her; and he did eat." In 1 Timothy 2:14, we see that Adam was held responsible for the sin that took place in the garden: "And Adam was not deceived, but the woman being deceived was in the transgression."

Female Characteristics

When God came to the garden after the transgression, He went to Adam first. God asked Adam, "Have you eaten from the tree of which I commanded you that you should not eat?" (Genesis 3:11). God didn't go to Eve; He went to Adam because he had been given the command by God and it was his responsibility to make sure it was obeyed. Looking at Adam's response, we discover a

---

[55] Ken Nair, *Discovering the Mind of a Woman* (Thomas Nelson, Nashville,1995), p. 35

male tendency that came about as a result of the fall. Rather than owning up to his failure, Adam pointed the finger at his wife and said, "The woman whom You gave to be with me, she gave me of the tree, and I did eat" (Genesis 3:12). Adam might have simply said, "It's your fault, God, for giving me this woman." So Adam refused to accept responsibility for his sin, blamed his wife, and actually blamed God.

This action by Adam shows the nature of men. They refuse to accept responsibility readily, but are quick to blame someone else for their failures.[56] Husbands need to understand that one of their primary roles is to protect their wives and children, both spiritually and physically.

Most people would be surprised to discover that many wives do not want to dominate in their marriages or homes. A wife generally wants her husband to be her spiritual leader, but she is designed by God to feel safe only when she sees her husband is not a dictator, but one who seeks the mind of God in all decisions. That is the only way she can feel secure that her relationship with her husband will be based on scriptural principles and not simply his own whims and preferences.

Often, the reproof of a wife is God's principal method of testing how Christlike her husband really is. As a responder, the wife will be tuned into the actions of her husband, and her responses will be a clear indicator of his spiritual condition, whether she realizes it or not.

Because men have a mechanical approach to life, they have trouble dealing with relationship issues with their wives. Husbands apply their mechanical solutions to the problems that develop between them and their wives. When their solutions do not work, they get frustrated and then withdraw. All of this points to the many differences between men and women and a desperate need for men and women to learn about these inherent differences.

---

[56] Ibid., p. 42.

CHAPTER 5

God's Order in the Family

Male

In the Genesis account of creation, the man is formed first, and then the woman. This sets the foundation for everything that will follow. God gave Adam the responsibility of naming all the animals and the command to tend the garden. He was given dominion over God's creation, and then God provided him with a suitable mate to help him accomplish all that God entrusted to him.

God laid out several things in the second chapter of Genesis: Adam was given responsibility to govern, to work, to shoulder responsibility, and to reproduce. We see that he was given dominance over all the animal kingdom and over all the earth (Genesis 1:26). Next, God told Adam to be fruitful and multiply (Genesis 1:28). God then placed Adam in the garden with the command to tend the garden (Genesis 2:8).

In Psalm 78:4, we see the responsibility of fathers to show to their children the things worthy of praise toward God. They were not to hide them or fail to share them with the children that will come after them. The praises of God, His strength, and

His wonderful works were to be constantly taught and reviewed before all the people. This was a commandment from God to fathers in order that the knowledge of God would be passed on from generation to generation.

The New Testament gives additional insight into the man's role as God ordained it. We read in Ephesians 5:23 the order of authority that God has established. The husband is listed as the head of the wife, and the wife is to submit to her own husband as unto the Lord.

As the head of the wife, the husband is to love her even as Christ loved the church and ultimately died for it (Ephesians 5:25). This command calls for a sacrificial relationship between the husband and his wife. The man has been given a leadership responsibility over his wife that demands protection, sacrifice, and devotion. First Timothy 2:12 warns against women usurping the authority given to the man and the following verse gives the reason: "For Adam was first formed, then Eve." This authority was stated very clearly in Genesis 3:16: "Unto the woman he said, I will greatly multiply thy sorrow and thy conception; in sorrow thou shalt bring forth children; and thy desire shall be to thy husband, and he shall rule over thee."

While God placed the man over the woman, it was a difficult position to be in. The woman became the object of the man's love, provision, and protection. The Lord understood the man, since He had created him, and He built into the woman all the traits and abilities she would need to accomplish her role.

Female

In Genesis 2:24, we read, "Therefore shall a man leave his father and his mother, and shall cleave unto his wife: and they shall be one flesh." The word translated *cleave* is very interesting as we look at the relationship between a husband and his wife. The Hebrew word is *dabaq*, "to cling, cleave, and keep close." Used in modern Hebrew in the sense of "to stick to, adhere to," *dabaq* yields the noun form for "glue" and also the more abstract ideas of "loyalty, devotion."[57]

God said it was not good for a man to be alone, so He created the woman (Genesis 2:18). Since God had already given authority to the man, it would be necessary for the woman to be able to adapt to the man, not compete with him for a leadership role. While God gave the man the necessary abilities to accomplish his role, He also gave the woman hers. Not only would she be able to adapt to the man, but God created her to be able to attract a man to herself and, through the one flesh experience, produce children. First Peter 3:1 states, "Likewise, you wives, be in subjection to your own husbands." Titus gives another clear statement as to the relationship and role of woman in God's creation. "The older women are to teach the younger women to be sober, to love their husbands, to love their children, to be discreet, chaste, keepers at home, good, obedient to their own husbands, that the word of God be not blasphemed" (Titus 2:2–5).

The ability of the women to be attractive is seen in the command to Timothy to make sure the women do not misuse this ability. Paul says, "In like manner also, that women adorn themselves in modest apparel, with shamefacedness and sobriety; not with broided hair, or gold, or pearls, or costly array" (1 Timothy 2:9).

We see that God has provided the woman with the ability to adapt to her husband, to attract a husband, and to bear children. Prior to the fall, there was no problem in this relationship, but after the fall, sin entered the equation, and conflict was the result. All of a sudden, there was the question of "Who is in charge?" The battle for control began with Adam and Eve and continues today.

---

[57] From *Vine's Expository Dictionary of Biblical Words* (Thomas Nelson Publishers, 1985).

Children

One of the first things God told Adam and Eve to do was to be fruitful and multiply (Genesis 1:22). After the flood, God repeated this command to Noah in Genesis 9:1: "And God blessed Noah and his sons, and said unto them, be fruitful." As we study scripture, we discover that God was the one who opened and closed the womb of women: "Lo, children are a heritage of the LORD: and the fruit of the womb is his reward" (Psalm 127:3).

The role of children is simple; children obey their parents in the Lord (Ephesians 6:1). However, it is the role of husbands and wives to train the children and prepare them to become adults who will repeat the pattern that God established, with the goal of filling the whole world with godly people. It is the responsibility of children to "hear the instruction of thy father, and forsake not the law of thy mother" (Proverbs 1:8).

How we approach life is in direct response to the philosophy of life we embrace. The Bible speaks of two philosophies in the world, the teachings of Jesus (theism) and the philosophy of the world (humanism). The two are distinct and at odds with each other. We read in Colossians 2:8, "Beware lest any man spoil you through philosophy and vain deceit, after the tradition of men, after the rudiments of the world, and not after Christ." Both of these philosophies are at work in this present age. These philosophies will have a direct impact on your life, depending on which one you chose to believe. They are not in harmony with each other, but direct conflict. The philosophy of humanism makes humans the center of all things. This creates a selfish attitude toward life: "what is good for me," "what can make me happy," and so on. Theism makes God the center of life, not ourselves.

Theism	Humanism
1. God is the **center** of all things	1. Humans are the **center** of all things.
2. Humans are the product of **creation** by God.	2. Humans are the product of **chance.**
3. Humans are **eternal** beings.	3. Humans are **machines.**
4. **Theological:** the Bible and faith (spiritual	4. **Secular:** science, sociology, the five senses awareness)
5. The universe came about by design and **creation** by God.	5. The universe came about by **chance** over millions of years.
6. **Increases** the value of human life.	6. **Decreases** the value of human life.

In Proverbs 8:36, we read, "All they that hate me love death." When we believe that life is precious and is a gift from God, it takes on value and meaning. If we believe that human beings are simply here by chance, then life is meaningless and is of little or no value.

Psychological Natures

The Male Psychological Nature

Created Traits

> Ability to exhibit
> Ability to shoulder responsibility
> Ability to reproduce
> Ability to work

Psychological needs

Dr. Norman Vincent Peale gave a lecture before a large audience and, at the end, opened up the floor for questions. A lady poured out her heart, sharing how she was doing all she could to make her marriage work, but her husband was not doing his part. Her question to Dr. Peale was this: "After twenty-five years of marriage is there any hope that he will change?"

Dr. Peale responded sternly and with passion, "Don't you know that you should always be willing to accept a man at face value and never try to change him?" The message to women everywhere is imperative: He must be accepted at face value. Don't try to remake him, or he'll become rebellious.[58] Not only do women's attempts to change their husbands, or any man, fail, but they often bring out a very real rebellion. This is the result of his attempt to hang onto his freedom.

He longs for admiration. The center of a woman's happiness in marriage is to be loved by her mate, but the main thing for a man in marriage is to be admired. It is true of every man: deep inside, he desires to have his wife admire him for the person he is. This admiration will lead to many different blessings for the woman in his life. As great as this need is, the man cannot achieve it alone; he needs his wife to provide it. A man often will show off in front of his wife in order to get some positive response from her, some admiration. Unfortunately, these things are often ignored or dismissed without the woman understanding what is being desired from her. Usually, a woman is too busy or too mentally drained by her own situation to respond. What the man wants is to be admired for his manly characteristics. Helping with the dishes is nice, but praise for that is not what is needed. The man needs to be admired for his masculinity, his strength, his courage, his sense of honor and duty, his leadership, and his judgment, to name a few things. And it is this realization of his masculinity that builds him up and excites his inner man toward the women who responds this way.[59] Don't be critical of him, or he'll become bitter.

He has a sensitive pride. A man's pride is very sensitive. Don't make fun of him; it will crush him. Men are natural show-offs. God created them with the ability to display the glory of

---

[58] Helen B. Andelin, *Fascinating Womanhood* (Pacific Press, California, 1972), p. 35.
[59] Ibid., p. 56.

God through their actions. Psalm 78:4–6 says, "We will not hide them from their children, showing to the generation to come the praises of the LORD, and his strength, and his wonderful works that he hath done." Men are to show their families what God is like by protecting them, providing for them, and loving them sacrificially, all illustrations of how God cares for His children.

He has a wall of reserve. When a man is made fun of or minimized, he will tend to build a strong wall around himself to protect against future attacks. When this takes place, the man will seem distant and removed. He will talk, but only in short sentences with limited details. The more he says, the more he can be criticized for. He will not openly talk because of his fear of more humiliation. If his confidence is taken away, he'll become withdrawn.[60]

He has sympathetic feelings. The main point is simply that men need to be taken at face value; they have a deep-seated desire to be appreciated for their manhood, and their pride is very sensitive. Men carry the burden of protecting and providing for their families. This responsibility of protecting and providing weighs heavy on most men, and its burden is not fully appreciated by many women. It is very easy for women to minimize these pressures and, in the process, cause the men in their lives to quit trying.[61]

He has a responsibility to fulfill. Don't steal his duties from him, or he'll become inferior. Just exactly what is a man's responsibility? From the first chapter of Genesis to the end of Revelation, we see man described by God as a guide, protector, and provider for his wife and children.

The man has been established as a guide to his family. God said to the woman in Genesis 3:16, "Thy desire shall be unto thy husband, and he shall rule over thee." Paul states that women are

---

[60] Ibid., p. 68.
[61] Ibid., p. 77.

to "reverence" their husbands (Ephesians 5:33). The apostle Peter tells women, "Ye wives, be in subjection to your own husbands" (1 Peter 3:1). In Ephesians 5, we see the man's leadership over his wife compared to that of Christ and the church. "Therefore, as the church is subject unto Christ, so let the wives be to their own husbands in everything" (Ephesians 5:23).

The role of protector is squarely on the shoulders of the man. All you have to do is look at the way God made and men and compare that to women. Men have more muscle mass, thicker bone structure, even more blood. In 1 Peter 3:7, men are told to dwell with their wives as with the "weaker" vessel.

The man's role as provider is seen in the first commandment God gave to Adam: "In the sweat of thy face shalt thou eat bread. Till thou return to the ground" (Genesis 3:19). This command was given directly to Adam, not Eve (Ephesians 5:33, Colossians 3:18, 1 Peter 3:1, Genesis 3:19, Ephesians 5:23–24).

God in His wisdom laid the responsibility on the shoulders of the man, but He also gave him what was needed to fulfill his responsibility. Man was created with the ability to handle the stress and strain of this responsibility, the capacity to make difficult decisions, and the strength and endurance to protect his family from all types of dangers. It is important to understand that a man desires to be superior in his role as a man. It is only in his role as man that he wants supremacy over his wife. He has no interest in being better than her in domestic items, or her position as a mother.[62]

While all men possess leadership tendencies, some have more ability than others. There are strong natural leaders, about 25 percent of the population. Most men are just average leaders, but every man has both the capability and the desire to be a leader, especially in his own home and marriage. This desire will result in some irrational behavior if it is not achieved. Again, we see a difference between men and women when it comes to leadership.

---

[62] Ibid., p. 90.

While some strong-willed women (cholerics) do enjoy leadership, they are in the minority. The majority of women would like for their husbands to take a leadership role, not as a dictator, but as a loving, strong leader.[63]

For most men, work is a compulsion. Productivity can even be a necessity. Deep within men is the God-given sense that is a necessity to work, to accomplish, to be productive. This is the way God created men. Genesis 2:5 says, "there was no man to till the ground," so God made man with this in mind. After the creation of man and before the fall, God placed man in the Garden of Eden "to tend and keep it" (Genesis 2:15). Man was created with the ability to work. There was and is no free ride, even before sin entered into the picture. After the fall, God's command to Adam was even more pointed: "In the sweat of your face you shall eat bread" (Genesis 3:19).

The first two children born on Earth are mentioned in relation to their areas of work: "Abel was a keeper of sheep, and Cain was a tiller of the ground" (Genesis 4:2). It was a long time before there appeared any confusion over the roles of men and women. Men were breadwinners, providers, and leaders of the home; women were to bear children and be "keepers at home." As a result of the confusion of roles, a number of problems have developed over who does what.

Another point that needs to be made is the difference between men and women when it comes to the idea of courage. All men have a basic ingredient to their makeup called courage. The amount will differ from man to man, but it is present in all men. It was this trait that made men the protectors of their families, homes, and countries. Courage is a trait both men and women possess, but they tend to show it differently. Women will courageously sacrifice themselves for their children; history is full of examples. When threatened, a woman may throw her body over

---

[63] Marlin Savage, personal notes (not published, 1976), p. 35.

her child to protect; not necessarily so with a man. He would be more inclined to engage in combat with the one threatening the well-being of his child.[64] It is this same spirit, innate courage, which sent Columbus to sea to discover the new world. It has moved many men to accomplish many heroic and amazing feats.

Believe it or not, even the mind of a man is different from that of a woman. In pursuing his role, it is necessary that a man think differently from a woman. This begins to show itself early in the life of children. It doesn't take long for boys and girls to separate themselves by their interests. Boys will gravitate toward cars, trucks, and sports items, while girls play house.

This difference is very clear in the area of sexual development. When a boy reaches puberty, he starts to develop physically as a man. He mentally cultivates an overwhelming interest in girls. At this stage of development, he is capable of sexual drives that women find difficult to comprehend.[65] Easily the most beautiful, fascinating, and intriguing sight in most men's eyes is a woman's body.

Another area that is different between men and women mentally is the man's goal-oriented thinking pattern. Women, by nature, tend to think vocationally of the home and the things that are a part of it, child rearing, and the needs of the family. Men tend to become absorbed in their vocational career pursuits. For a man, his means of livelihood can easily become the focal point of his life, especially if he likes his work. The result is that his home life suffers, and he may even neglect fathering his children properly at crucial times in their lives. A man needs to periodically take an objective look at his children and occasionally restructure his priorities in order to meet his family's needs.

On the emotional level, men tend not to be as strongly influenced as women of the same temperament, but they still have strong feelings. All of us have feelings; they are not spontaneous, but

---

[64] Ibid., p. 41.

[65] Ibid., p. 43.

the result of your thoughts and activities. If your thoughts are good, good feelings will soon follow. Do you want to change your feelings? Then change your thoughts, and gradually your feelings will change.

While men have a sex drive that generally confuses women, women have a capacity for love and affection that is greater than men's. The strength of a woman's emotional feelings is far beyond most men's comprehension. Men need to learn to do what comes naturally to women: show love and affection on a regular basis.

Behind every man's complex nature is a little boy. Sooner or later, the little boy will show himself in public. Some men are practical jokers; others just love excitement. Some think they are still capable of being on the high school football team. Some think the beltway is their own personal racetrack. This trait in men drives them to seek out some form of excitement. For some, it is contact sports, hunting, fishing, or some other form of competition. Fathers love to give their kids toys that they can play with themselves. It may be hard for wives to understand, but the boy in every man is what makes him a sports lover.[66]

The Female Psychological Nature

Created Traits

> Ability to adapt
> Ability to attract
> Ability to reproduce

Psychological Needs

To understand that the psychological needs of a woman are different from those of a man requires only for a man to get married. Within a very short period of time, the man will discover

---

[66] Ibid., p. 52.

that his wife does not respond to things the same way he does. Things that are of no major concern to a man may well create major concern for a woman. This difference is both a problem and a blessing. If the man will work at understanding the psychological needs of his wife, their marriage will benefit in many ways. These differences will balance the marriage relationship, with each providing a unique contribution that the other lacks.

She needs to be loved. Don't forget to tell her you love her, or she'll feel worthless. A survey was conducted to understand what ingredients make for a happy marriage. When the results were in, the answers were predictable: "All we need is love." Most men know this to be true, but doing something about it is the difficult part.[67] The love that women crave is really dependent more on a sense of protection. Women need to know that they are protected at all times, from everything. If they believe they cannot trust their husbands to protect them, it is difficult for them to sense that their husbands love them.

The results of this survey were very interesting. No matter where couples live and regardless of economic or social standings, there are amazing threads of commonalities that run through all marriages. Here are some of the results:

- People seem to have the same problems in their marriages, no matter how long they've been married.
- No one has a perfect marriage.
- Husbands are quite transparent and knowledgeable about their inadequacies.
- Wives, by and large, are forgiving of their husbands, but also recognize their husbands' faults clearly.

---

[67] Hans and Donna Finzel, *The Top Ten Ways to Drive Your Wife Crazy* (Victor Books, 1974), p. 23.

Without a doubt, there is a common thread when it comes to the top issue that creates conflict and difficulty in marriage: a woman's need for love.

Love is the issue, and love is the key for women. But love for a man is very different from the love that women want and need.

A number of men were asked the following question: "What do you think is your wife's number one need that you should fulfill?" The answers were predictable:

"Two words sum up her greatest need: *affection* and *attention*."

"She needs my encouragement by paying complete attention to her."

"She needs my continual love and acceptance."

"She needs to be cherished, not just through words (although they are critical), but through thought and deed."

This is a small sampling of the responses, but enough to make a point. There is a recurring theme of love and affection that is recognized over and over. Unfortunately, though an equal number of men were surveyed as women, only the women responded in mass. Men were either not interested or too busy to respond, especially when the questions had to do with such an often-guilt-ridden area.[68]

To most women, affection symbolizes security, protection, and approval. When a husband shows his wife affection, he sends her the following messages:

"I'll take care of you and protect you. You are important to me, and I don't want anything to happen to you."

"I'm concerned about the problems you face, and I am with you."

"I think you've done a good job, and I'm proud of you."

Interestingly enough, a hug can say all of the above. Men need to understand how strongly women need these affirmations. For the typical wife, this part of her relationship is of major importance. Men need to understand that they must pay attention

---

[68] Ibid., p. 23

to these needs. Most women love to hug; they hug each other; they hug children, animals, relatives, and sometimes stuffed animals.[69]

She needs to be complimented. Don't overlook her femininity, or she'll attract others. God has given the woman the ability to attract a man. This is necessary to lure a man away from home. This ability never goes away and is a part of a woman that needs to be understood. But many men fail to see the necessity of meeting the need of their wives to feel attractive. Just as strength is part of a man's makeup, attraction ability is part of a woman's. Women have a basic need to feel secure, part of which is the compliments of her husband. When a man compliments his wife, he is telling her that she is still attractive to him. This compliment assures the wife that she is safe from the possibility of another woman attracting her husband away.

She needs to be respected. Don't reject her ideas, or she'll feel incompetent. Some men take the position that they are the kings of their castles and they are the only ones capable of making any decisions. As a result, they smother their wives and lose the benefit of their perspective and insight. God's has balanced the husband-wife relationship by giving each a special ability and perspective. The wife is the counterbalance to the husband, pointing out details that men often overlook or ignore. When a man refuses to give an ear to his wife, he is diminishing his effectiveness and causing emotional stress to his wife.

She needs security. Don't ridicule her feelings, or she'll become frightened. Ridicule is always cruel, but it is particularly cruel when it is directed by a husband to his wife. Men should be constantly looking for ways to protect their wives. When a man stoops to ridiculing his wife, he becomes the adversary. When this takes place, the woman begins to seek protection elsewhere. If this continues over any length of time, a psychological division will develop between the man and the woman that may never heal.

---

[69] Willard F. Harley Jr., *His Needs Her Needs* (Fleming H. Revell, 1994), p. 34.

She needs gentleness. Don't be unkind to her, or she'll seek it elsewhere. This is where the male masculinity needs to be aware of female tenderness. Open doors; give a gentle touch, a soft caress, and soft words. We are told to deal with our wives as the weaker vessels (1 Peter 3:7). Women cannot and should not compete with men on a physical basis. Treating a woman with tenderness sends the message, "I value you and want to protect you." This is another way of making a woman feel safe from the world.

She needs your presence. Don't refuse to be with her, or it will make her feel unwanted.[70] One complaint that women share on a regular basis is the lack of time they have with their husbands. After the wedding ceremony, the pressure begins to build concerning finances. The household needs fall on the man, and in the early years, just getting by is a struggle. As a result, men will often work overtime or take a part-time job. The man feels good about all the hours he is working to provide for the family, but the wife gets upset because the extra hours or extra job simply take him away from home and away from her. While the woman may understand the need for more money, her emotions create a conflict within her. The rational understanding sometimes gets lost in the emotional struggle against feeling unwanted by her husband. Her thoughts move toward the idea that "If he really cared for me, he would find some way to spend time with me."

Here are some practical applications for men. Husbands need to know that affection is the glue that will hold your marriage together. To most women, affection symbolizes security, protection, comfort, and approval—all vitally important items in their eyes. When a husband shows his wife affection, he is providing a key ingredient for a successful marriage.

Remember, protection means she is important.

---

[70] Ibid., p. 66.

Listening intently shows a concern for her personal problems: "I am with you."

Compliments are essential for her to feel self-esteem.

She can never get too many hugs.

Men need to understand how strongly women need these affirmations. For the typical wife, there can never be enough of them. Hugging is important, and most men need to develop this skill. It is important for men to realize that for women, affection does not automatically lead to sex. There are times they just need to be held, period. There are, of course, other ways of showing affection: a greeting card or note describing your love for her, flowers, an invitation to dinner. Do not forget holding hands, walks together after dinner, back rubs, phone calls. There are a thousand ways to say "I love you," and remember, creativity counts.

Affection is so important to women that they become confused when their husbands do not respond when women offer it to them. For example:

She calls you at work just to say she was thinking of you, but you cut it short because you are busy.

She writes little notes and puts them in your travel bag, but you do not acknowledge them.

She wants to hold your hand when you're out shopping, but you don't want to be bothered.

> Almost all men need some instruction on how to become more affectionate. In most marriages, a man's wife can become his best teacher, if he approaches her for help in the right way. First, tell her you love her, but you want to know what conveys that to her in the best way. She may be surprised at first, but after she has a chance to think about it, she will be very helpful. The first ten minutes after a husband gets home from work

each night are critical. They will set the tone for
the rest of the evening with his wife.

Typically, a man will come home after a long day at work and just want to crash. The wife, having waited all day for his return, wants to engage him in conversation. She wants to know how his day went, what he did, and how he handled things. The man, having just gone through all of that, does not want to rehash it again. This lack of sharing sends the signal to the wife that her husband does not want her to be a part of his world. The man is simply happy to be home but fails to understand the need of his wife for dialogue.

CHAPTER 6

God's Creation and Sin

The Effects of Sin on the Male

The effects of sin are universal, whether one is saved or unsaved. There is a price to pay for each and every sin committed; however, not everyone responds to temptation in the same way. When confronted with temptation, a sanguine would not react the same as a melancholy temperament. So, if we look at the effects of sin on our individual personalities, we will see that the sanguine and choleric temperaments will go in one direction and the melancholy and phlegmatic temperaments will go in the opposite direction.

Dr. Tim LaHaye, in his book *Your Temperament,* states,

> Self-understanding is only one benefit gained from knowing the theory of the four basic temperaments. In addition, it helps you understand other people, particularly those close to you. Many a matrimonial battleground is transformed into a neutrality zone when two individuals learn to appreciate their partner's temperament. When you realize that a person's actions result from temperament, rather than being a tactic designed

to anger or offend you, this conduct is no longer a threat or an affront."[71]

There are some basic principles that we can recognize and apply. For one, opposites do attract to each other. What could be more opposite than male and female? A negative is never attracted by another negative, and positives repel each other in any field: electricity, chemistry, and particularly with temperament.

What is it that attracts one person to another? "Usually it is the subconscious recognition of and appreciation of their strengths."[72] "If given enough association with the person who sparks our attraction, we experience one of two things. Either we discover weaknesses in them similar to our own and are understandably turned off by them, or we discover other strengths we are lacking, which translates admiration into love."[73]

What turns you off to other people often is simple the fact that the two of you may be too much alike. Like temperaments seldom cohere. A sanguine would seldom marry another sanguine; both are such extroverts that they would be competing for the same stage in life, and no one would be sitting in the audience. Sanguines need an audience to turn them on. Cholerics, on the other hand, make such severe demands on other people that they not only wouldn't marry each other, but probably would never date—at least, not more than once. Two melancholies might marry, but it is very unlikely. Their analytical traits find negative qualities in others, and with this being said, they would never pursue each other. Two phlegmatics would rarely marry, for they would both die of old age before one got steamed up enough to ask the other one to marry. It is very possible that they could go

---

[71] Tim LaHaye, *Your Temperament* (Fleming Revell, Grand Rapids, Michigan, 1977), p. 209
[72] Ibid., p. 211.
[73] Ibid., p. 211.

steady for thirty years and never say, "I love you"; they are that protective of their feelings—they rarely let them show.

While each temperament is different, there are still basic principles that apply to each of them. To understand how sin has impacted the human race, we need to start with the first sin recorded for us in Genesis 3:6: "She ate, and gave also to her husband, and he did eat." The effects of sin on the individual abilities can be seen in the response of Adam and Eve to God's question, "Did you eat of the tree, whereof I commanded thee that thou shouldest not eat?" Adam responded to God, "The woman whom thou gave to be with me, she gave me of the tree, and I did it," (Genesis 3:12*).* From that moment on, Jeremiah 17:9 applied to all men: "The heart is deceitful above all things and desperately wicked, who can know it?"

The Ability to Exhibit

Because of sin, the ability to exhibit resulted in men who were extroverts (sanguine and choleric) becoming proud and selfish, developing an exaggerated opinion of themselves, and becoming jealous, suspicious, egotistical, and boastful. Proverbs 16:18–19: "Pride goeth before destruction." Second Timothy 3:2: "Lovers of their own selves, covetous, boasters, proud." Uncontrolled sin resulted in these types of men becoming self-worshiping, mean, mercenary, and idolatrous.

However, men who were melancholy and phlegmatic tended to go to the other extreme and become inferior, deficient, falling short, secondary, second rate, lethargic, withdrawn, failures, grouchy, grumbling, and complacent. In 1 Kings 21:1–7, King Ahab is an example of this type of response. The end result was indifference, lack of caring, unresponsiveness, and no desire to please others or to be liked.

The Ability to Shoulder Responsibility

The sanguine and the choleric will move toward becoming dictatorial, narrow-minded, intolerant, superior, egotistical, conceited, opinionated, unreasonable, dogmatic, and critical. An example of this can be found in 1 Kings 12:12–14 with Rehoboam and in Daniel 4:1–37 with King Nebuchadnezzar. This response results in a large amount of hostility, arguments, impatience, anger, war, and murder.

The other end would be the melancholy and phlegmatic developing a very submissive attitude, showing up as being dependent, relying on others, tending to follow, being fearful and insecure, and seeking peace at any price. Illustrations of this are found in Isaiah 19:16, Nahum 3:13, and Jeremiah 50:37 and 51:30, where we read that men become as women! All of this resulted in men becoming inactive, uncontrolled, and disorganized.

The Ability to Reproduce Himself

The ability to reproduce is also impacted by sin. When the command of God to have one man with one woman for life is set aside, the result is devastating. The sanguine and choleric will move toward an immoral life, full of evil thoughts, lasciviousness, uncleanness, lustfulness, and promiscuousness without natural affection (Galatians 5:19; Proverbs 6:23–29). The result is uncontrolled adultery, polygamy, and homosexuality.

The melancholy and phlegmatic will appear to move in the opposite direction, but basically will end up at the same place. They will project a prudish manner with false modesty; they will become hypocritical, insincere, unnatural, hypercritical, inhibited; they will split hairs, act delicate, and become hard to please (1 Corinthians 6:9, womanlike).

The result is a strict, strait-laced appearance but will end with a homosexual lifestyle, if left unchecked.

The Ability to Work

The effects of sin can also be seen in the area of work. The sanguine and choleric will tend to move toward being greedy, covetous, cheating, stealing, grasping, prone to extortion, mercenary, stingy, grudging, and gluttonous (James 3:14–16; Luke 12:15, beware of covetousness). This will result in a display of envy, strife, and selfish ambition in relationship to anyone who gets in their way.

The melancholy and phlegmatic will go in the opposite direction, resulting in a lazy approach to life, often being very inactive, idle, slothful, dull, procrastinating, drowsy, a bum, lazy, unoccupied, unemployed, and a slacker (Proverbs 24:30–34). This person will spend every opportunity to sleep, slumber, and generally do nothing, resulting in extreme poverty.[74]

The Effects of Sin on the Female

The Ability to Adapt

Like the man, the woman will respond based upon her temperament. The ability to adapt is a critical part of a woman's makeup and essential in the well-being of a marriage. God created the woman with the purpose of assisting her husband, helping him become all that God intended him to be. However, when sin entered the picture, the ability to easily adapt to her husband become a real challenge.

For the sanguine and choleric temperaments, allowing the sin nature to control them would result in the woman becoming a domineering force. Her desire would move toward ruling over her husband in direct opposition to her role. Paul, writing to Timothy, said, "But I suffer not a woman to teach, nor to usurp authority

---

[74] Tim LaHaye, *Why You Act The Way You Do* (Tyndale House, Wheaton Illinois, 1984), p. 62–78.

over the man, but to be in silence" (1 Timothy 2:12). In Proverbs 7:11, we see how sin can affect the behavior of a woman: "She is loud and stubborn; her feet abide not in her house." Proverbs 19:13: "The contentions of a wife are a continual dropping." Proverbs 21:9: "It is better to dwell in a corner of the housetop, than with a brawling woman in a wide house." Proverbs 21:19: "It is better to dwell in the wilderness, than with a contentious and an angry woman." The result will be a matriarchal society, where women dominate the will of society. In Isaiah 3:12, we read that when women rule over men, it is a sign of God's judgment.

With the melancholy and phlegmatic woman, the results tend to be the opposite. When they are caught up in sinful behavior, they tend to gravitate toward being gullible and accepting everything without question. We find a description of this type of woman in 2 Timothy 3:6: "For of this sort are they which creep into houses, and lead captive silly women laden with sins, led away with divers lusts." Paul warns Timothy to "refuse profane and old wives fables, and exercise thyself rather unto godliness" (1 Timothy 4:7). This type of woman has a tendency to move toward superstition and idolatry (Jeremiah 7:18; Ezekiel 13:17–23). If left unchallenged, it will result in an occult society where false religions and cults prevail.

The Ability to Attract

The sanguine and the choleric become bold and show a lack of restraint when their sin nature is allowed to dominate. They easily will become very forward, with no sense of modesty—very bold, forward, shameless, and indecent. First Timothy 2:9–10 describes how a godly woman should present herself: "In like manner also, that women adorn themselves in modest apparel, with shamefacedness and sobriety; not with broided hair, or gold, or pearls, or costly array; but (which becometh women professing godliness) with good works." First Peter 3:3–4 says, "Whose adorning let it not be that outward adorning of plaiting the hair, and of wearing of gold, or of putting on of apparel; but let it be the hidden man of the heart, in that which is not corruptible, even the ornament of a meek and quiet spirit, which is in the sight of God of great price." Isaiah 3:16–17 is very clear: "Moreover the Lord saith, because the daughters of Zion are haughty, and walk with stretched forth necks and wanton eyes, walking and mincing as they go, and making a tinkling with their feet: therefore the Lord will smite with a scab the crown of the head of the daughters of Zion." This is a command against immodest dress or appearance and extensive use of ornaments.

Proverbs 7:10 and Ecclesiastes 7:26 talk about being subtle and deceitful. Proverbs 2:16–20, 5:3–14, 6:20–35, 7:6–23, and 9:13–18 all deal with being evil, lewd, and seductive. The result is adultery, prostitution, pornography, and homosexuality.

The melancholy and phlegmatic, once again, will tend to go in the other direction. For this group, their sin nature will lead them into a lifestyle that is careless, negligent, and untidy, generally taking no care of their houses or themselves. A woman in this category just lets herself go. Her person is disorderly. Her home is a mess, with "long green hairy stuff growing in the refrigerator" (Jay Adams). We find a description of this woman in Isaiah 32:9–11:

> Rise up, you women that are at ease; hear my voice, you careless daughters; give ear unto my speech. Many days and years shall you be troubled, you careless women: for the vintage shall fail, the gathering shall not come. Tremble, you women that are at ease; be troubled, you careless ones: strip you, and make you bare, and gird sackcloth upon your loins.

Isaiah 47:7–9 gives another harsh account of what God will

do to those who refuse to take care of their responsibilities the right way:

> Therefore hear now this, thou that are given to pleasures, that dwellest carelessly, that sayest in thine heart, I am and none else beside me; I shall not sit as a widow, neither shall I know the loss of children: but these things two things shall come to thee in a moment in one day, the loss of children and widowhood: they shall come upon thee in their perfection for ht multitude of thy sorceries and for the great abundance of thine enchantments.

The end result for this group of women is a lazy and indifferent lifestyle, where they live in the world of the soap opera.

The Ability to Reproduce Herself

The ability to reproduce and provide godly children who will in turn grow up and produce godly children is greatly impacted by the sin nature. The sanguine and choleric will move toward becoming busybodies; they are unable to stay out of other people's business. First Timothy 5:13 mentions idleness, wandering from house to house; also 1 Kings 10:31—misguides her own children (Jezebel.) The result is a person who interferes in the lives of others and is prone to gossiping and backbiting. Proverbs 18:8, 20:19 and 26:20–28 all warn about the results of gossiping.

For the melancholy and phlegmatic woman, we see a person who just lies around the house refusing to tend to anything. The end result is a woman who is neglectful, one who is lazy and unproductive. This type of woman will refuse to have children or simply let her children care for themselves. If she does have children, she will often simply forsake her children—no regular meals, clothing left in piles, dishes stacked on the counter, children dirty, etc. The main result: this type of person is usually a flirt, is fickle and has a very poor, undesirable household.[75]

The Effects of Sin on the Total Personality

The effects of sin on the total personality is also known as "the male-female conflict," the first of four basic conflicts involved in every marriage.

The Male

We need to go back to Genesis 3:12: "The woman whom thou gavest to be with me, she gave me of the tree, and I did eat." What we see here is that Adam failed to fulfill his created responsibility.

He failed to display the glory of God to his wife.

He failed to rule over (guide) his wife.

God responds to Adam's sin in Genesis 3:6; 3:17: "Because you harkened to your wife …" God held Adam responsible for the first sin. Even though Eve ate first, Adam was at fault for failing to protect her from herself. The result of Adam's action is a male tendency to pass the buck and blame someone, anyone, when caught in failure. This tendency can be seen very often in the workplace. At home, this can be devastating because the wife is usually the closest one to her husband, and she is made the scapegoat of his blame; this is a very common cause for divorce.

The result of Adam's action is a judgment from God. He is given increased difficulty in work, a major role in his life (Genesis 3:17–19). In addition to increased difficulty in work, Adam is now given even more responsibility for his wife (Genesis 3:16; Ephesians 5:22–31; 1 Corinthians 11:3–9; 1 Timothy 2:11–15).

---

[75] Ibid., p. 87.

The Female

The female also did not escape responsibility for her part in Adam's sin. It is interesting to look at the judgment God laid on the woman. When God spoke to Eve concerning what she had done, her response was classic, in Genesis 3:13: "And the woman said, 'The serpent beguiled me and I did eat.'" Even though Adam should have stopped Eve, she was still held accountable for what she had done. Eve failed to fulfill her created responsibility. First, she failed to adapt to her husband when Satan came. Secondly, she submitted to the weakness of her nature. Noted in 1 Peter 3:7 and 1 Timothy 2:14, "as unto the weaker vessel." This resulted in a female tendency to plead helplessness, sit down, and shed a few tears when caught in failure, which in turn has an effect on the husband—it melts and dissolves his determination and effectiveness in ruling over his wife. Thus, this diverts attention from the failure or problem. The husband is confronted with a hurting spouse instead of one who needs to face accountability for her actions.

Eve's improper response resulted in being cursed by God (judged): increased difficulty in childbearing, a major role in life (Genesis 3:16), increased submission to her husband (Genesis 3:16; 1 Corinthians 11:3–12; 1 Corinthians 14:34–35).

The Effects of Sin on the Work Ethic

The effects of sin on the work ethic are also known as the "curse of work," the second of four basic conflicts present in every marriage. These conflicts arise over provisions for the family and the methods used to obtain them.

1. God cursed the source of supply:
   a. Cursed is the ground for thy sake (Genesis 3:17–18).
   b. The whole creation groans and travails in pain (Romans 8:18–25).

2. God cursed the attitude toward work:
   a. In sorrow shalt thou eat of it (Genesis 3:17).
   b. I hated all my labor, which I should leave it to another (Ecclesiastes 2:18–26).

3. God cursed the man's body:
   a. In the sweat of thy face shalt thou eat (Genesis 3:19).
   b. If any would not work, neither should he eat (2 Thessalonians 3:7–15).

4. God cursed the lengths of time:
   a. Until you return to the dust (until death, Genesis 3:19).
   b. His breath goes forth; he returns to the earth (Psalm 146:4).

This conflict can best be handled in the family by avoiding demands on the husband's income for "extras", avoiding conflicts of interest between family members, and helping each other when the "curse of work" begins to get you down.

The Effects of Sin on the Presence of Children

The effects of sin on the presence of children are also known as "the problem of children," the third of four basic conflicts present in every marriage where there are children. When children are present in a marriage, problems arise over the bearing, training, schooling, dress, friends, activities, etc., of the children.

God planned for men and women to bear children and enjoy their offspring. Satan's plan is to fill the Earth with ungodly, unthankful, unruly, and depraved people. His plan begins with the children. The presence of sin has made childbearing more difficult. The "one flesh" experience is the method for conception, and until recently, it was the only method (Genesis 2:24; 4:1, 25). Early in the history of humanity, we see God's plan being replaced: Genesis 4:19 describes the advent of polygamy. God's judgment included making conception and birth more difficult (Genesis 3:16). This judgment involved multiplied sorrow and multiplied pain (labor pains) in childbirth.

Not only are problems increased in childbirth, but after the arrival of children, additional problems are created. Some of the new challenges involve the restrictions on living spaces, finances, freedom, and lifestyle. In addition, there are the problems of the population explosion, physical deterioration of the body, and just plain weariness experienced by parents. Psychological problems also arise, including confusion, depression, and strain (the need for more space, the question of discipline, what friends to allow, and of course, what college the children should attend.)

Sin has made child-rearing more difficult. One responsibility of parents is to teach their children about God (Genesis 4:2–4; Proverbs 6:20–23). The problems are what to teach the children and when and how to discipline them. The methods used to teach and to correct often create conflict between parents. Plus, the nature of being the parent and being the child are in conflict (Genesis 4:5–12). Proverbs tells us that foolishness (rebellion) is bound up in the heart of a child (Proverbs 22:6, 15; 29:15, 17; 23:13–14; 19:18). We are given the action to take against absolute rebellion in children in Deuteronomy 21:18–21.

> If a man have a stubborn and rebellious son, which will not obey the voice of his father or the voice of his mother and that, when they have chastened him, will not hearken unto them: then shall his father and his mother lay hold on him and bring him out unto the elders of his city, and unto the gate of his place; and they shall say unto the elders of his city, this our son is stubborn and rebellious, he will not obey our voice; he is a glutton and a drunkard. And all the men of his city shall stone

him with stones, that he die: so shalt thou put evil away from among you; and all Israel shall hear, and fear.

Of course, this is not possible today; however, it does show the seriousness of the attitude God places upon discipline. Parents are responsible to do everything possible to control the actions of their children.

The conflict is often due to inconsistency on the part of the parents (Ephesians 6:4). God's solution to the problem is to seek wisdom from the Lord (Psalm 127:1–2). The parents are to give children instruction from God's word (Deuteronomy 31:12–13) and, when needed, apply the "rod" in corrective discipline (Proverbs 1–3, 7, 13:24).

The Effects of Sin on the Family's Life

The effects of sin on the family's life are also known as the "plague of worldliness," the fourth of four basic conflicts present in every marriage. Setting up a home and its related problems are the source of many conflicts. God's plan for the family (Genesis 2:8–15) is that humans might live in communion with God. Satan's plan for the family (Genesis 3:22–24) is to develop a world view contrary to God's.

The life of Cain and his family shows us this earth-oriented life, which should be a constant concern for the Christian family. It occurred in downward steps. Cain left God out of his life (Genesis 4:16); Cain went out from the presence of the Lord. Even today, Christians do this all too easily. In Hebrews 10:25, we are warned about forsaking the gathering together of believers; there is the tendency to believe that we do not need God in our daily lives.

Cain established a pattern for those who want to live apart from God; he put down roots. In Genesis 4:17, we are told that he built a city, and later his followers built a tower (Genesis 11). Today, we are consumed with things: buying houses, collecting things, etc. The one who has the most toys at the end wins! Whatever happened to God's idea of His people being pilgrims and strangers (1 Peter 2:11, 1:17; Hebrews 11:13)?

Most people are so tied to this world that when God calls, they can't move. We can see how those who followed Cain centered their lives on temporal things. Fleshly pleasure became the main goal for many: "Lamech took unto him two wives" (Genesis 4:19). If one is good, two is better! Possessions became important; the accumulation of things marked the level of success in a worldly environment: "The father of such as have cattle" (Genesis 4:20).

The seeking after amusements was needed to fill their spare time: "The father of such as handle the harp and organ" (Genesis 4:21) Things, activity, and the accomplishing of projects dominated their thinking: "Instructor in the forging of brass and iron" (Genesis 4:22).

The natural result is the glorification of sin, polygamy (Genesis 4:23), and murder (Genesis 4:24). For the natural man apart from God, there is a movement toward a "goal-oriented" life that leads away from godliness; Genesis 6:5 declares that man's every imagination is evil continually. Such people become victims of their own affluence (Proverbs 30:7-9). God's solution to this problem is found in Genesis 6:8: "But Noah found grace in the eyes of the Lord." The grace of God is available to all who seek Him. In Exodus 33:12, we read that Moses spoke to the Lord and said, "Now therefore, I pray thee, if I have found grace in they sight, show me now thy way, that I may know thee, that I may find grace in thy sight: and consider that this nation is thy people." God responded to Moses, and He will do the same for us.

God has called all men to be just (Genesis 6:9, Job 2:3). Genesis 6:9 says we are to be blameless in our generation. Genesis 6:9 *also* tells us that we are to walk with God, the same way that Job did (Job 1:1).

CHAPTER 7

Concluding Observations

Our Choices

The one thing that stands out most in this study is the fact that people make choices and those choices have consequences. Beginning with Adam and Eve and following throughout the entire Bible, we see how choices have created specific results and problems. Adam's choice not to stop Eve from eating the forbidden fruit has impacted every person who has ever been created. The result has been a constant struggle for people to deal with the fact that God holds us all accountable for our actions and those actions can produce blessings or curses.

The Bible gives us a blueprint for life, and at the center of this is a call to love the Lord with all our hearts. This is followed by the call of Jesus to love our neighbors as ourselves. These commands are clear, though difficult at times to fulfill. God has also called individuals to specific responsibilities, and when those responsibilities are followed, the individual, the family, and the community all prosper. When humans fail to put God first by seeking to fulfill their God-given responsibilities, everyone suffers.

If anyone will seek to establish the priorities that God has laid down in His word, that individual will find meaning and purpose in life. The family unit will be blessed, and the community will be better off. Many men have fathered children, but not all of them have been good fathers. The world has seen many ruthless, mean, and treacherous dictators come and go. The fact is that most, if not all, have had poor fathers who failed to love, instruct, and discipline their children in a biblical manner.

The Bible tells us that "Foolishness is bound up in the heart of the child and the rod of instruction will drive it far from him (Proverbs 22:15)." It also says, "He that loves his son will chasten him (Proverbs 13:24)." Susanna Wesley understood this truth when she dealt with her children (all seventeen, to be exact), two of whom turned England upside down for God. "The child that is not taught to obey their parents in the home will neither obey God or man outside the home" (Susanna Wesley).

Our Consequences

We have seen generations come and go that basically ignored biblical principles. Personally, I have witnessed four decades of biblical neglect by parents, resulting in a generation of undisciplined, unholy, unthankful, spoiled, self-indulgent, and rotten people. Serving as a pastor and counselor over the last forty years has given me firsthand evidence of a decline nationally, in the family unit, and personally among individuals, all of which points to the fact that biblical truth needs to be understood and applied in our daily lives in order to maintain a good quality of life. The consequence of ignoring biblical truths is creating a society of self-centered people who suffer from high degrees of stress, fear, and hopelessness. They lack direction and a purpose in life. The only way to find fulfillment in life is to realize our purpose: to honor and glorify God in everything we do.

Bibliography and Credits

Adams, Jay E. *Solving Marriage Problems* (Baker Book House, Grand Rapids, Michigan, 1983).

Blamires, Harry. *The Christian Mind* (Servant Publications, Ann Arbor, Michigan, 1997).

Crabb, Dr. Larry. *Inside Out* (NavPress, Colorado Springs, 1998).

Eavey, C. B. *Principles of Mental Health* (Moody Press, Chicago, 1975).

Finzel, Hans and Donna. *The Top Ten Ways to Drive Your Wife Crazy* (Victor Books, a division of Scripture Press. 1986).

Gray, John. *Men Are From Mars Women Are From Venus* (Harper Collins Publishers, New York, 1992).

Harley, Willard F. *His Needs Her Needs* (Fleming H. Revell, a division of Baker Book House Publishers, 1992).

Keirsey, David. *Please Understand Me* (Promietheus Nemesis Company, Del Mar, California, 1984).

Kennedy, Dr. D. James. *Why I Believe* (Word Publishing, Dallas, Texas, 1980).

Kilpatrick, William, *Psychological Seduction the Failure of Modern Psychology*, (Thomas Nelson Publishers, Nashville, Tennessee, 1983).

LaHaye, Tim. *Your Temperament: Discover Its Potential* (Tyndale Publishers, Wheaton, Illinois, 1983).

LaHaye, Tim. *Understanding the Male Temperament* (Fleming H. Revell, a division of Baker Book House Company, 1996).

LaHaye, Tim. *The Act of Marriage* (Zondervan Corporation, Grand Rapids, Michigan, 1976)

LaHaye, Tim. *Why You Act the Way You Do* (Tyndale House, Wheaton, Illinois, 2000).

Logan, William. *In the Beginning God* (Adult Christian Education Foundation, Madison, Wisconsin, 1985).

Malkmus, Dr. George H. *Why Christians Get Sick* (Destiny Image Publishers, Shippensburg, Pennsylvania, 1995).

McMillen, S. I. *None of These Diseases* (Fleming H. Revell, Grand Rapids, Michigan, 1995).

Rogers, Adrian. *Ten Secrets For a Successful Family* (Crossway Books, Wheaton, Illinois, 1996).

Wangerin, Walter *As For Me and My House* (Thomas Nelson Publishers, Nashville, Tennessee, 1973).